W9-ADH-770

The Classmates

ALSO BY GEOFFREY DOUGLAS

Class

Dead Opposite

The Game of Their Lives

HYPERION
NEW YORK

The Classmates

Privilege, Chaos, and the End of an Era

Geoffrey Douglas

ISBN: 978-1-4013-0196-5

Book design by Richard Oriolo

Hyperion books are available for special promotions, premiums, or corporate training. For details contact Michael Rentas, Proprietary Markets, Hyperion, 77 West 66th Street, 12th floor, New York, New York 10023, or call 212-456-0133.

FIRST EDITION

10 9 8 7 6 5 4 3 2 1

"[It] had been like a paradise that I had to leave, like Adam had to leave the garden. It was just too perfect. In a few years' time a shit storm would be unleashed. Things would begin to burn. Bras, draft cards, American flags, bridges, too . . . The road out would be treacherous, and I didn't know where it would lead, but I followed it anyway . . ."

—Bob Dylan, from *Chronicles: Volume One*

Contents

Author's Note

THIS BOOK HAS BEEN AN EXERCISE in reconnections: to a group of classmates I hadn't seen or thought of in decades, an unhappy time I had tried to put behind me, a young self it still pains me to recall. A part of me dreaded the process of writing it; I just didn't want to go back.

But a strange thing happened when John Kerry, a classmate, ran for president in 2004. His candidacy set off a domino-chain of classmates' emails—which was understandable enough. The voices in these emails, though, or in many of them, were not ones I could bring into alignment, no matter what allowance I made for the passage of time, with the boys whose faces I still saw behind them. And I began to question myself.

Then came a second event: another classmate, a very different sort of classmate from John Kerry, died unexpectedly. His passing brought more emails—and these were even more foreign to me: touched with an honesty and a tenderness, and ultimately a sense of shame (for there was much to be ashamed of in the case of this boy) that seemed unimaginably at odds with the classmates I recalled.

My questioning then grew into something like a quest—which, in the end, is what this book has been for me: a connecting of old ghosts with their real-life, latter-day voices; and later, with the hearts and minds and life-stories that have made these voices so different and so real.

The process began with many voices—forty or more—and over time was winnowed to fifteen or so, and finally to seven (including myself and the classmate whose death unlocked such rawness). It is to these five other classmates, with whom I have spent so many hours over the past three years, that I owe my first and largest debt: for their time, their honesty, and, above all else, for their trust. These are men, without exception, who had not seen or heard from me in more than forty years, yet were willing to share with me some of the most private—and sometimes darkest—chapters of their lives. Over months of long lunches and dinners, and the emails and phone calls in between, I listened to stories of love, war, death, business, marriage, divorce, depression, sexual identity, alcoholism, abstinence, and a hundred other things. And from these stories—together with my own, those of our lost classmate, and briefer glimpses of others—I have worked to fashion a wider story: of a piece of a generation and a particular moment in time.

So, for their honesty, courage, and the trust they invested in me, I need particularly to thank John Cocroft, Chad Floyd, Philip Heckscher, John Kerry, and Lloyd MacDonald.

My deep thanks go also to Louise Friend, whose love for and deep appreciation of her brother filled for me gaps that would have left this book thinner by far.

There were many classmates, in addition to the five named above, with whom I spent time, either personally or on the phone; and others whose emails added importantly to my story. Principal among these were: Dan Barbiero, Chris Chapin, Geoffrey Drury, Bert Myer, Sean O'Donoghue, Seymour Preston, Tip Sempliner, Bill Tilghman, Wick Rowland, and Bill Wallace.

Thanks also to Will Schwalbe, for having the vision to see this story in the first place; and to both him and Brendan Duffy, for seeing it through. Also to Tim Rodd for his insights on boarding-school life.

And to Sam, my editor-son, who plowed his way through at least two renditions, and was as kind as he was helpful in the suggestions he gave—that's a real gift of yours, Sam. And to Christine, for her advice and abiding friendship. And my good friend Mel, whose lifetime of editing served me almost as well as his humor and support.

Printed sources of particular help have included: *St. Paul's: The Life of a New England School,* by August Heckscher; *Tour of Duty: John Kerry and the Vietnam War,* by Douglas Brinkley; and *John F. Kerry: The Complete Biography,* by staff reporters of the *Boston Globe.*

Which leaves only Landon to thank. And I don't have the words for that. Her support, her patience, her love, and her faith were oftentimes all that kept me typing.

The Classmates

Familiar Strangers

The boy sits on the toilet in the center of the half-frozen meadow, bolt upright as we pass. He is fully clothed and zippered—wearing the same stained trousers and jacket we will see him in every day and night for a week—his feet planted an inch deep in the muck, the smile on his face so dumb and unmoving it seems almost to be carved.

"I recall there was a thin layer of ice on the water," one of us, our class president, will remember in an email decades later. "It is a truly painful memory. It was painful even then."

The boy is fifteen or sixteen, like the rest of us, but different in almost every other way. He is bigger by far: six-foot-two or -three and well over two hundred pounds, with broad, nearly square shoulders and the short, thick neck of a dockworker or heavyweight wrestler. His clothes are a joke among us: fifteen-dollar polyester blazers from Sears or Robert Hall, trousers that stop an inch short of his ankles, heavy brown, mud-caked oxfords that never get shined or changed. Everything about him is a joke: his clothes, his helmet haircut, his caveman's rolling shuffle, the hard, white stains on the crotches of his pants. But we are careful with our laughter, because his temper is volcanic and he is stronger than any two of us.

His name (the name I will call him) is Arthur. It is said that he is from a farming town in Pennsylvania, that he has come to the school on a scholarship, and that he has been "all the way" with a girl—in the back of a hay truck, as the story is always told. There is a rumor that he once righted a tipped car singlehandedly to free the driver inside, and another that he is physically afraid of his father (which conjures images of a family of Goliaths). But it is hard to know what is true. He seldom talks about himself (in contrast to the rest of us, for whom self-talk is a daily staple), and almost never talks at all when there is a group around. But he will sometimes explode into laughter—a sudden staccato chain of throaty roars, like a man choking on his dinner—for what seems no reason at all. Beyond these few things, and his enormous size and strength and uncouthness, he is a mystery to us all.

We have paid him to be on this toilet today. Someone *has paid him: fifty cents or a dollar or maybe a little more, because he will do almost anything for three or four quarters (he will do worse than this before his time is done at the school) and because quarters, or dollars, mean nothing to the rest of us. And someone has dragged out this junkyard toilet from somewhere and hauled it to the meadow and set the time and spread the word around the dorms: "On the way to chapel Sunday—another Arthur show."*

So he sits now in the meadow with his feet in the icy mud and smiles his dumb, determined smile. And the rest of us file past, slowly, in clusters, on our way to breakfast or to Sunday evening chapel—it might have been either one, a gray April morning or the dying light of a Sunday late afternoon, and too many years have passed now to say which—adjusting neckties, buttoning shirt collars, whispering and gawking and ready to laugh.

But no one laughs. Or almost no one. And what laughing there is is thin and nervous, and dies just past our throats—its memory years later will bring pain. A few of us look away.

The sense of wrongness spreads quickly, like a bad smell coming to ground. We walk faster—all eyes averted now—until the boy and his toilet are behind us and out of sight.

THE FIRST THING I DID WHEN the photo came to me, by email, from a classmate I hadn't seen in more than forty years, was to count the faces in it. There are 105 of them—of *us*—as nearly as I can tell, lined up raggedly, more or less by height, all of us in jacket and tie, on the steps of the St. Paul's School auditorium. We are fourteen years old; a few of us are fifteen. Almost no one is smiling. We are a very somber group.

I am in the front row: shoulders flexed back, head cocked to one side, feet spread wide—James Dean or Elvis, or a gunslinger—next to my best friend, Rich DeRevere, a scholarship student with a buzz cut who will be a radio reporter and the father to a girl and a boy, then will die in a Florida hospice at the age of sixty-one, a year before I will know he is gone. There is mowed grass in the foreground, wide white columns to our backs. It is a weekday afternoon in the fall of 1958.

Once I'd counted the faces I began to study them. I studied them for hours, one by one and in clusters, enlarging then reducing, going up and down the rows, until an afternoon and an evening had passed.

There are the timid ones, who bunch their shoulders or shrink behind others; the swaggerers and the lip-curlers (I am one of these) whose sad, shallow bravado still hurts a little to see on record today; the sullen ones and the serious ones and the ones with the goofy looks. And there are those, even at fourteen—Lloyd MacDonald, blond, square-shouldered, and taller than the boy to either side, who will be our senior-class president; Bob Mueller, future hockey-team captain and head of the FBI; Peter Johnson, brainy and irreverent, who will be named editor of the school's literary magazine, then will die outside a Vietnamese city called Qui Nhon—who seem already to have mastered the secret, of never seeming to try.

It puzzled me why I felt so drawn to the photo. It wasn't one I remembered; I remembered almost no photos at all. I had been expelled from St. Paul's a year short of graduation, at the end of my fourth year there—breaking a long family tradition with what my father would call the "stigma" of my disgrace—and my memories prior to that had not been happy ones. I owned no yearbooks, had never attended a reunion, had kept up with no one in the class. Yet I could tell you at least something about every face in that picture, and I remembered nine-tenths of the names. And I kept going back to it. For all the confusions and small remembered terrors those faces stirred in me, I kept on going back. I still do.

It's been more than two years now—I understand better today what it is that keeps drawing me back. There is a strangeness that comes, for me at least, in looking at old photos. A sadness mixed with wishfulness, a mixing-up of time. To look backward from here to there, but also, by looking back, to *be* there again, only now to be looking forward: to know that this boy would thrive and that boy wouldn't, that this one would climb vertically, almost unimpeded, while that one would have terrible troubles, that the level-eyed calm of a boy in the back hid a secret, that the vivid talents and visible sureness of another would be squandered in an early death. There is something intrusive in the feeling, but also seductive, like looking through a door left open by mistake.

JOHN KERRY IS IN THE FOURTH row. He is one of the serious ones: lips pursed, eyes furrowed, head tilted a little awkwardly to avoid being obscured by the boy in front of him. (He would graduate, four years later, among the tallest in our class, though he was still, at the time, among the shortest.) It's hard to know what he might be thinking. He looks, for the moment, perplexed.

He is the reason, today, that I have the photo at all. It came to me by way of a classmates' email group that formed the spring before the 2004 election, originally to share reactions to a magazine story that appeared around that time. Headlined "John Kerry, Teen Outcast," it had opened with an account of John being booed, in absentia, at our fortieth St. Paul's reunion, then gone on to detail how reviled he had been at the school ("Forty-two years after the fact, many of his classmates still mock him . . . They dislike him so much they've frequently helped his political opponents.").

I don't know how true any of this is. I don't know if he was booed at that dinner or not—Lloyd, our president, who gave the toast that allegedly drew the boos, swears that he wasn't—or how many of our classmates have continued to hate him with such feeling. It's hard to get most of them to say anything at all about John. Some claim to be gun-shy from being misquoted by reporters who called before the election (probably a third of the class got such calls, in search of school-day remembrances); others just smile and shake their heads when I ask them, or go suddenly quiet on the phone.

But whatever anyone's feelings on John today, it's fair to say that, as a classmate, he wasn't widely liked. Nor was he any sort of leader in the class. So it is ironic, these many years later, that he would be the one to unite us again.

But it has happened that way. The email group, which began as a handful of classmates with that single small focus, quickly took on members and widened its scope: first into a discussion of the campaign and its chances, later to the values behind it ("I would vote for John whether I liked him or not . . . ," "My heart is with John, [but] my conservative instincts haven't really changed much since our school days"), and finally to other, less political things. Through the summer, then fall of 2004, there were emails on Iraq, gay marriage, the economy, school prayer, flag burning, God, woodwinds, Bob Dylan, the Yankees, the Red Sox, a hundred other things. By the weekend before the election, more than two-thirds of us still surviving—fifty-odd late-middle-aged men in at least four different countries and something like twenty states, some not having talked to a classmate in decades—were getting and sending messages at a pace of twenty a day.

I would never have expected this. I don't know what I would have expected, probably something not so different from the pabulum of life-landmark highlights

I'd read from time to time over the years in the school's alumni magazine ("After nineteen wonderful years working as X and living in Y, Susie and I have decided to close out this rich and rewarding chapter in our lives . . ."). But this was nothing like that—it was better, braver, richer by far. It felt kind of magical, at least for a while: like stepping through a door back into that photo, trading voices, hearing echoes, sharing our astonishment at having evolved.

As the weeks passed—first before, then after the election—the messages grew more personal. Old memories were reprised and recast; there were exchanges on work, family, failed relationships, art, music, creaky knees, the creepage of time and age. One classmate wrote in to recall, among other things, an old English teacher's epic nose-blowings ("He would pull out from his tweed jacket sleeve a large handkerchief, would unfold it ceremoniously, blow loudly, then return it with great dignity to his sleeve. It's what I remember most about third-form English."), another to share his recollections of "the peace, the quiet grace" of Sunday evening chapel. Two classmates, both former marines, recalled aspects of their time in Vietnam. A journalist from Connecticut wrote to share the news of his father's recent stroke and death. A lawyer from Maine, whom I remember mostly for his withering sneer and mirror-shined English loafers, told of how religion had reentered his life after law school ("I wonder for how many of us our religious education has proved to be important?"). A doctor from the West Coast wrote to tell of an early life of depression, drug use, and multiple divorces: "But I've emerged into my sixties in pretty good shape . . . very much a lightweight in terms of planet accomplishments compared to some of you, but have found an appreciated niche here in [my community] and in my children's hearts. And that will do."

The most prolific, by far, was Arthur. Arthur the hulk, the toilet-sitter, the class jester and pariah; Arthur of the filthy, crud-stained fifteen-dollar suits and revolting public hygiene, who would suffer any debasement for a fistful of quarters, was now a salesman of mobile-home parts in western Virginia: alone, never-married, and nurturing—incredibly—an abiding fondness for his long-ago school.

"You all have offered a lot of stimulating and good and kind thoughts in our exchanges about Kerry and other matters," he wrote the week of the election. "A number of remarks about myself were forwarded to me on the general topic of the 'gentle giant' . . . I thank you for your extraordinarily kind remarks, which I probably did/do not deserve."

I must have missed those early "gentle giant" messages—though there would be many more like them in the months to come. But his emails were a deluge. They began two or three weeks before the election and continued until more than three months after. I don't know how many there were—twenty, thirty, maybe more, sometimes two or three thousand words at a time—about politics, sports, business, integrity, encyclopedia sales, his sick mother, his early life. The messages were impassioned, often embarrassingly personal. He wrote of an illness that had nearly killed him two years before, and of the resolve he said had grown from it: "to make things a little better while we are here, and to improve our eternal characters for whatever may come beyond." He leaned heavily on clichés—also on allegories—cited self-help books, quoted Vince Lombardi, and referred more than once to The Creator. He seemed driven by the need to connect.

"I have decided that this discussion group merits some of my quality time for several reasons," he wrote in a February 2005, late-night email. "I can learn and share with other privileged and smart people—just as I can, and have, with those much less so. I wish to change the world for the better, though the odds of doing a lot of that are dicey. In the meanwhile, I can continue working on myself and who knows where some of the sparks of that effort may fly."

Most of us ignored him. When someone would respond, Arthur would write back promptly—to us all. "Thank you for caring and responding," he'd begin. Then would come the monologue ("Suppose you are an astronaut . . ."). When someone would try to rein him in, which happened more than once, his response was always benevolent: "One classmate has good-naturedly pointed out that I can be long-winded. Guilty, no doubt. Perhaps turgid and bloated, too. At least I hope to be credited as a forthright searcher for higher truth."

He was lonely. That much seems clear. Also that he

had forgiven us—if he even felt any longer (but how could he not?) that there was anything still to forgive. I used to wonder this sometimes. We must all have wondered it, at one time or another during those three or four months of what he liked to call his "epistles": How does he remember us? How could he share himself so nakedly given the degradings he suffered at our hands—cruel jokes and hazings, public humiliations for which he'd be paid several quarters or a dollar to endure? Or had he managed somehow, in his need for connection, to forget that they even took place?

One of the ways he had earned his quarters, especially during our first year or two at the school, was as a kind of enforcer. If you had a score to settle with someone, or just were looking for a spectacle at the expense of a boy you didn't like, you might engage Arthur for the job. I was at the wrong end of this once. I have no memory of why I was the target, or of who had contracted for Arthur's muscle that day; what I remember is being grabbed by the arm on the way out of the lower-school—eighth-grade—dining hall, dragged in a headlock upstairs to the third-floor fire escape, and either pulled or pushed through. Arthur came through with me, got hold of my lower legs, picked me up, and tossed me—literally *tossed* me, as you might toss a rug for cleaning—over the fire-escape railing, where he held me by my ankles twenty feet from the ground. I remember that his palms were wet against my bare skin, and that, although I was certain he wouldn't drop me on purpose, I was terrified he might lose his grip. I held very still, said whatever it was I was made to say—"I am a fairy," "I am a homo," "I promise I'll . . . ," there must have been something—then was lifted back over the railing, set right-side-up and let go. Through it all, Arthur never hurt me or was any more forceful than he needed to be, though his strength was greater than any I had felt in my life. I remember feeling that he wasn't enjoying my terror; he may have even told me so. He may have even smiled, or said something gentle or consoling, before he set me free.

Forty-seven years later, a week or so after the 2004 election, I sent Arthur a long email, which included my fire-escape remembrance. He wrote back a day later, assuring me, as I'd expected, that he had no memory of it. His message then concluded:

"If I did something as reckless as your memory indicates, I do earnestly apologize, even at this late date. Yes, I remember I was quite often 'over the top' in those days, but do honestly regret if I put your life and limb in danger. I am glad to hear you are well."

ON THE NIGHT OF NOVEMBER 2 the Kerry campaign lost the election. The emails over the next several days were subdued. ("I'm quietly depressed this morning, but certainly not without hope.") Most of our group, probably as much for reasons of common history as anything else, had come around to John's side by the end—although there were some vocal exceptions. ("I have been badgered by journalists over the last several months . . . I can't stand the guy and don't want anything to do with him.") Over four or five days in mid-November, a collective email to the defeated candidate was drafted, amended, agreed to, and sent:

> Dear John:
>
> We are many of your classmates from the St. Paul's School form of 1962. From across the political spectrum and around the world, we write to express our deep admiration and heartfelt gratitude for the honesty, integrity, spirit and reason you brought to the presidential campaign . . .
>
> Your candidacy has also produced another consequence . . . It has, literally, brought much of the form together after more than 40 years . . . and resulted in the renewal of decades-old friendships. For all this too, we thank you . . .

My name was among the signers. Arthur's, too, I believe. There were about sixty names in all. One of the original drafters was a boy with a flat-top haircut in the second row of the photo, now a broadcast executive in the West. Most of what I remember about him is that his dorm room smelled of after-shave and that he had an odd, kind of motionless walk.

But to look at him now in the photo, looking out

fixedly from between the shoulders of the boys in front of him; then to read the email, his email, written to the boy three rows behind him who will almost be president but who, for now, is only a short, befuddled fourteen-year-old trying hard not to be effaced by the boy in front of him—is like being pulled back into an old, familiar dream. One of those dreams you wake from but still feel holding you, till you break free by force of will.

They are all strangers to me. Familiar strangers. Even the ones I knew better. Even my best friend Rich, standing there next to me with his big ears and his stoic, shoulders-back posture (he's the only one in the front row whose hands remain behind him): I knew about him only that he was uncommonly kind, generally unafraid to show his feelings—both dangerous qualities at St. Paul's in those days—quiet, unathletic, almost slavish in his studies, and either mocked (*"DUH-DUH-DUHHH-Revere!"*) or ignored by nearly every boy in the class. Also that he sometimes borrowed my neckties because he was ashamed of his own, and that he smelled always of the coffee he consumed by the gallon day and night. Beyond these things, almost nothing. And since then, nothing at all. Only facts.

Even me. There I stand in that ridiculous, spread-legged, curled-lip self-parody of a pose—"You had an *attitude*," a friend says in looking at the photo today. But what attitude exactly? Who *was* that boy? Out of what insecurity or lopsided teenage value came that gunslinger's swagger that day?

I don't know. I remember him, of course. I remember some of his fears and feelings, some of what he might have been trying to hide behind that day. I remember that he often felt angry, that he seldom walked when he could run (his nickname was "Dash"), and that he talked far too much and bragged sometimes about things he'd never done. I remember him as I remember Rich or Arthur or the after-shave wearer—far better than them, though in just the same way. But I can't touch him. I can't reconstruct him. I don't know where he went.

Where did *any* of us go? And who were we, really, even then? And what were we trying to prove today—composing this tribute of "deep admiration" to a boy we only half-remembered and mostly didn't like? Or extolling, for his "gentleness," a boy who revolted us when we weren't sitting him on toilets for quarters or dropping booby-trapped buckets of water on his head? Or writing emails about our stricken parents, our religious wonderment—as though we'd known each other our whole lives?

It is only memory that gives us this privilege. The thin familiarity that comes with remembering things: that this boy was a terror on the hockey rink (as John came close to being, though what's best remembered is that he seldom passed the puck), that that one was a bookworm, or a prankster, or was said to be a "homo," or had the best dates for Dance Weekend, or kept a stash of Newports under a rock by the Lower School Pond. These are the credentials we carry of our classmates, the worn little legacies that creak with disuse when we go to unlock them, then fall apart at the first suggestion of today.

PART OF IT COMES FROM THE sharing of just having survived. St. Paul's was a hard place in those days. And we were young and far from home. Even apart from our cruelties to each other, apart from the loneliness and homesickness and the austere, even forbidding surroundings we shared, it was a life meant to harden and deprive. "Tough and nasty" is how one classmate describes it in an email. "We were an elite in the matter of leaving childhood early, and learning how to take the pain."

Almost no one, I think, would have called himself happy. The mornings were too early, the work too hard, the daily regimen too punishing, the winters too endless and cold. The isolation was oppressive, and purposefully enforced: a phone call required a quarter-mile walk followed by a fifteen-minute wait in line; a trip into town was layered with bureaucratic compliances; overnight absences, except for family emergencies, were not allowed at all. There were, of course, no girls.

There was nastiness everywhere. Public humiliation was part of the currency we shared. Grades were posted publicly; misbehavings were announced by the headmaster—the rector—before morning meetings of the school. In the classroom, if you gave a wrong answer to the wrong teacher—"master"—you were apt to receive a stick of chalk to the head. "*If your brains were dynamite,*" he would shriek at you, his face twisted in contempt, *"you wouldn't have enough to blow your nose!"*

Disobedience was unthinkable. An upperclassman, during my second- or third-form year, famously defied chapel dogma, at several successive services, by facing the wrong way during the reading of the Apostles' Creed; one morning, very quietly, he was gone. Violations of the Honor Code, understood by every boy to be sacred—the supreme commandment of life at St. Paul's—were grounds for instant expulsion (so terrifyingly so, at least to me, that for two years, obsessively, I rewrote every page of every homework paper that betrayed any sign of an erasure or mistake).

There were many cliques, but only one that ever counted. The Regs—for regular guys—dressed in Brooks Brothers suits, French cuffs, and gold pin-collars, spoke their own private language, and carried their derision the way a beat cop might carry a nightstick. Their cruelties were ingenious, and extended to every corner of the class. There seemed no social or public dimension—how you dressed, walked, talked, ate, played, and studied; who your friends were; which way you blew your nose—for which the standard wasn't unassailable, and hadn't been set by the Regs. They were our Mafia.

(One classmate, who had come to St. Paul's from a middle-class town in suburban New York, would recall for me later an incident that occurred his first week or two at the school: "I had my jacket off and my sleeves rolled up—most of the way to my armpits, the way I'd rolled them all my life. And [one of the Regs] came up to me: 'No, no, no,' he said. 'We don't roll our sleeves up like that here. We only roll them up three times.'")

But beyond and above all this—and underlying it—were two absolute precepts of life. The first was *manliness:* you never complained or made excuses, or said your likes or longings out loud. The next was *Christianity.* The message of each—of both—seemed stitched into every prayer and plaque and saint's statue, every chapel homily, every hockey game and homework assignment, every minute of every day. ("Behave in life as a game and clean man behaves on the football field," Teddy Roosevelt had written in 1917—the same year my father had arrived as a third-former—in a note to the school that remains framed there in a hallway today. "Don't flinch; don't foul; and hit the line hard.")

There was no pity anywhere, and no softness. For all the slavishness to Christian teachings—the eight-times-a-week chapel, the psalms and scriptures, the weekly sermons on our missionary duties to the poor and oppressed—there was very little comfort given, and not an ounce of Christian love in sight. (Only once in four years did I see a boy cry publicly. It happened on the soccer field. The coach ignored it; every boy nearby, including me, moved away.) We were stalwart little soldiers. We worked hard, competed furiously in everything, kept our tears and terrors to ourselves, and stepped cruelly and publicly on anyone—such as Arthur—who could be seen as misfitted or weak.

It had been this way, allowing for small swings in culture and leadership, for a hundred years already, since a twenty-six-year-old Latin tutor and Episcopal minister, Henry Augustus Coit, had been named the first rector of the school, with twelve boys under his charge, in the fall of 1856. Very little had changed, and nothing basic—the elite, all-male student body, the enforced isolation, the classics-based curriculum, the Spartan ethic, the eight-times-a-week chapel—between that time and the time of my father in the early 1920s, or between my father's time and mine.

"I pray that every St. Paul's boy will remember that he is a gentleman," Henry Coit had told his charges, in a sermon sometime around 1890, addressed to the school on the eve of a summer's vacation: "This school does not stand for the hotel manners popular at the seaside; this school does not stand for turning night into day, nor for morning hours lolling in bed, nor for the desecration of the Lord's Day now becoming so common."

AS THE WEEKS PASSED AND THE emails grew more honest and more interesting to read, I began to pay real attention—first to the themes of what was being written, then to the writers themselves. I began to try to match the one with the other, to link the messages I was reading—of work, family, loss, the beginnings of decrepitude—to the sixteen-year-olds I once had thought I knew. Some of the pairings seemed likely enough; others were harder to see. Still others seemed unthinkable, beyond imagining.

I'd find myself rereading an email, then enlarging the image of its writer in the photo on my screen, trying to make the one fit the other. I couldn't stretch my picture of the boy with the cruel mouth and the shiny loafers into a seeker after meaning and faith—yet it seemed that he'd become one. I couldn't conceive of the undersized, wise-ass drummer I'd roomed next to leading a platoon of marines in Vietnam. Lloyd, our president, had gone on to a career as a federal judge, which seemed fitting, even predictable; and John, whose lust for the limelight had been a class joke even then, was today a senator. But a boy who'd seemed to care about nothing so much as his Vitalis-slicked hairstyle and his closetful of Brooks Brothers suits (whose trousers he sometimes wore under his shin guards to hockey practice in an exhibit of disdain) was now a high-school history teacher who wrote understated emails about the value of friendship and the disappointments of parenting. And Arthur had forgiven us, and was now apologizing for himself.

It amazed me, all of it. It captured me. I began sending more messages of my own. I got into a dialogue with an old dormmate, now a businessman in New York—we would eventually meet there for dinner, though I would never see him after that—who recalled for me his view of things, a year out of college and still carrying the secret of his gayness, on shipping out for Vietnam: "Maybe I'll just get shot and no one will have to know."

Another boy, now a bookbinder and retired financial planner and among the shyest, most solitary members of the class, wrote to me of a life lived much the same way. ("Essentially, I am a recluse à la Emily Dickinson, but without the genius. And I like it that way.") Some wrote mostly of their careers or business successes. Some stuck to politics. A few wrote back to share their memories of me: "Remember the practice we gave to three-man football? The plays, with Bert and Weaver, that we could call out on the line, on cue, and run the likes of Bobby Mueller to the ground?"

I'd forgotten those games, until he reminded me. His name is John (like at least eight others in the class); he was small and fast, as I was; we probably made a good team. Today he works for a marine shipping company in San Francisco; I never heard from him after that. The gay Vietnam veteran shared a large room with another boy in the dorm I lived in my last year at the school; I used to go there some nights to play backgammon for quarters and listen to "Runaway."

The more we wrote, the more I remembered. The more we all must have remembered—that's what the emails were about. One of us had just run for president and nearly won. The face that had filled our TV and computer screens all those months had been the face of a jumpy, over-driven boy, whose questings had been too crude and naked to suit us but had taken him, nearly, to the fulfillment of an impossibly daring dream. To remember him now was to remember ourselves: our own boys' questings, how much we had dared for them, what fruit they had or hadn't borne.

"We were all shot from the same gun in June 1962," a classmate would write in an email not long after the election. "Some of us have flown straight, some at a tangent, some have missed the target entirely . . ."

I wasn't one of those shot from that gun. It was a different, most would say lesser school that would grant me my diploma that year. But that's almost not a difference at all. We finished—wherever we finished—in June of 1962. John Kennedy was in the White House. John Glenn was the biggest hero since Lindbergh. *Happiness Is a Warm Puppy* and *Sex and the Single Girl* were what most of the country was reading. The sixties—what we would come to know as the sixties—were still three or four years away.

We finished college, most of us, four years later. That was the year James Meredith was shot on a freedom march in Mississippi; there was a race riot in Watts and peace marches in New York and Washington. So the changes were beginning—but only just. It was still the time of folk songs and high ideals: Joan Baez, Peter, Paul and Mary, Timothy Leary, Lenny Bruce. A hippie was still a flower child; a protest march could still be a Walk for Peace and Love and Freedom; a policeman wasn't yet a pig. It hadn't turned angry yet.

"By '66, it was getting to the point where you could see it coming, that you were going to have to come down on one side or the other," another classmate, later a marine officer in Vietnam, would tell me over lunch the summer after the election. "It wasn't in your face yet at that point, but it was getting there."

The next year we bombed Hanoi and the war's body count nearly doubled. There were riots in Detroit and Newark, peace vigils in Washington, draft-card burnings in Central Park. Then the Tet Offensive—February '68—and the riots spread to the campuses; then King and Robert Kennedy, both dead inside two months. Then the Chicago convention with its macings and clubbings; and two thousand deluded romantics carrying Vietcong flags, teargassed in the Capitol while several thousand more walked in circles around the White House carrying candles and singing for peace.

"The top blew off," the old marine would tell me. "It just blew, pretty much overnight. It was never the same after that."

This was the stage we arrived on, then departed from—for first jobs, grad schools, the Peace Corps, Vietnam—to make our ways in the world. We were smart, privileged, wonderfully well educated, more than half of us at Ivy League schools. We were the cream; we were the future (and had been told so, by how many commencement speakers on how many broad green lawns); we would carry the hopes of our schools, our families, and our country ahead into a perilous time.

And a lot of us did. But some of us stumbled, and some are stumbling still.

I've been one of the stumblers. Along with enough

others to make up a pretty fair share of the class: the West Coast doctor who tells of his depression and divorces, a retired Hollywood writer come and gone from five different careers, the Vietnam veteran who struggled so long with his gayness, the bookbinder who writes that "the real world and I have never seen eye to eye." And a New York artist, also gay, who suffered a breakdown trying too hard to be his father's son. And a former alcoholic from Rhode Island, another Vietnam vet, who will open his life to me. And Arthur. And four or five others I'm not as sure about. (Plus the stumblers, however many, who haven't come forward as stumblers or haven't joined our group at all.)

It's a tricky thing to make judgments about failure and success. And there are, of course, no sure gauges. But the more emails I read—and as time went on, the more lunches and long afternoons I would share with their writers—the more it began to seem to me that, as a group of classmates, at least in the early years, we had stumbled and backslid more than most.

The war was a big part of it. It decided a lot of things. Some of us enlisted, others got drafted (most of these eventually found their way to Vietnam), while many of the rest, who might have hoped to be artists or bankers or to bump around a year or two, instead chose routes that would keep them from the draft: law school, a teacher's job, the Peace Corps, or VISTA. By the time the war ended, the choices had congealed: the law-school grads were lawyers by then, the teachers were teachers for life. One classmate, with law school already behind him, signed on for a year-long stint with VISTA, working with Oklahoma Indian tribes, to get himself past draft age ("the magic, undraftable twenty-six," he would write later in Princeton's alumni magazine). Seven years later, still living on a Cheyenne reservation in Montana, he was counseling the locals on small-business affairs: "Some myths had been exploded. [I had found] the moral imperative to make efforts to improve what I saw."

But the war was only part of it. There had been a shift. The rules had changed just as our game got started. For four years at St. Paul's—and another four, for most of us, at Yale, Princeton, Williams, Amherst, or Brown—we had played and studied hard, dressed neatly (and uniformly), deferred to authority, upheld tradition, and come to understand, almost by osmosis, that there were responsibilities that attended the accident of our birth.

Then everything got flipped. In the space of not much more than a year, a lot of the old root work, the old icons and assumptions, got ripped apart and recast. (The tipping point is hard to place exactly, but it was sometime in 1967, around the time most of us began living life for real.) Authority and tradition were suddenly invidious. Nine-to-five was a failure of the imagination. Money and privilege were somehow obscene. Teenage boys burned their draft cards ("Hell No, We Won't Go"), and dared the police to arrest them; young women gathered publicly to mass-incinerate their bras. It was that year or the next that they put suffixes at the end of "elite."

It was a giddy time—that was most of the point. But

it was also unbalancing. Where before there had been a system with rules and a road map, there was now a strange sort of vacuum. In place of yesterday's clear expectations was now a frighteningly open road. We had been schooled, more than most, in obedience, respect, and emotional forbearance. All around us now were defiance, irreverence, and unthrottled feelings and drives. Reaching back for those years—'67 and the three or four years that followed—the strongest echo that comes to me is the sense of feeling lost.

SOME OF THIS SAME ECHO, THIS memory of lostness, was coming through in the emails: the classmate who confessed he'd rather have died than been outed, the doctor's memories of depression, the naked loneliness of Arthur's late-night rants. The more I read, the more I found myself asking: How did that boy become this man? How many of the stumblers, and which ones, had found sure footing—and where, and through what, had they found it? And what had caused us, back then such stingy, cloistered, tough-minded little WASPs, to be today so sharing of ourselves?

Had it mattered that we'd read Caesar and Virgil and the Hellenic wars? Or studied Paul Tillich and the Letters of St. Paul, and sat in chapel every morning and twice on Sundays for four years? Had the St. Paul's Honor Code taught us anything lasting about honor? Were we stronger, more abiding people for having carried the weight of following in our fathers' paths? And all that intellectual rigor—were we smarter, more penetrating thinkers for having learned, at sixteen, to parse an argument?

I didn't have the answers, if there were answers. All I had was the sense I got, and still get, every time I look at that old photo: that for all the hope and pride and tradition, and all those thousands of tuition-dollars spent, the world we were groomed for at St. Paul's in 1959 was more orderly by far, and more forgiving, than the world we were to find.

"SPS was a bastion of that whole preppie, 'Episcocrat' thing," my marine classmate would say to me at the end of our lunch together. "They trained you for it, the same way they'd been training kids the last eighty or ninety years, the same way they trained some of our fathers, like yours . . .

"Then it all blew up in our faces—BOOM! Gone, just like that."

Shame

In a minute or two he will come. My "coach"—that's what he calls himself. He will come with his stained white mug of gooey black coffee brewed on the little machine in his room (he says it must always be black, with the grounds still at the bottom, if I expect to get results) and will turn on the swivel-lamp on my desk and point it straight in my face. Then he will find my ankle under the covers and yank it, hard, then cup his hands around his mouth and do his reveille imitation—"pa-PA-pa-de-RUP/pa-PA-pa-de-RUP"

—and slap the desk and hiss: "Up and at 'em!" or "Rise and shine!" or something else just as idiotic.

It is five-thirty in the morning and snowing. I can see it outside my window, falling slow and straight against a blueberry sky. Other than Rich's slapping and blowing, and the background clank of the radiator down the hall, the dorm is as quiet as a church. It is more than an hour till the wake-up bell—though Rich, I know, has been up at least since five. He's dressed already in the same clothes he'll wear to breakfast, minus the jacket and tie, and smells of coffee and soap.

I hate these mornings. But I've promised him not to complain. I've promised to get up when he wakes me and to be at my desk by quarter to six at the latest, then again by nine at night. I've promised to share with him the notes I'm taking in classes—to prove I'm taking them at all—and to submit to his quizzes anytime that he asks. I've promised, for this one "fortnight" (the name for a marking period, roughly five weeks, at St. Paul's), that I'll trade my sloppy habits for Rich's way of doing things. Neither of us has said much about what will happen after that.

It is February 1960. Two months ago I finished the first half year with a grade-point average of sixty-eight—including an F and a D. A week ago, on the way back from Greek class, where I'd just failed another test, I asked Rich what he thought the chances were that they'd flunk me out of the school. (I'm sure that's how I put it: "You think they'll flunk me out of school?") But it wasn't a real question, and he knew it—I was probably grinning when I asked. And he stopped dead on the path, turned to face me, and said, "You make me sick."

I asked what he meant. He said that I should know what he meant. He said that I was smart, that I was smarter than he was, that he had to slave for the B's and C's he made (and he does slave, he really does, like almost no one else in the form), and that I spent my nights reading dumb novels and listening to records and writing letters to girls—and that yes, I'd probably flunk out and I probably didn't even care. And the whole thing made him sick.

I was embarrassed. No one ever talked to me like that before. I said he was wrong; that I do care. (And it was true, I do. I only pretend that I don't.) He told me to prove it. I asked how could I prove it. He said I could work hard the same way he does, that I might even come to like how it feels. I said I wouldn't know; I'd never worked that hard before. He said that if I was serious he could help me, that he could be a kind of "coach." I thought about it for a while, then said okay—but only for a fortnight, I told him, I couldn't promise after that. He said that that was fine with him. So we made up some rules, and that's how we came to our deal.

So now he comes every morning with my coffee, and again every night to make sure I'm at my desk. On the evening visits, he'll give me little quizzes—if I have some test coming up—or check my homework if I don't. Then will come a last visit, just before lights-out: "Good job," he'll say when he finds me still at my desk. "You've got that Greek vocab down really solid," or, "You're going to ace that algebra test." Then he'll pat me on the back just like a coach would, and tell me again for the five hundredth time: "Just keep thinking—'Shot From Guns!'"—after the cereal ad slogan that's always on the radio. Then he'll turn off my desk lamp and tell me to go to sleep. And I will.

In the end none of it will matter. I'll raise my average nearly ten points that fortnight (including a twenty-point improvement in Greek), and Rich and I will celebrate in his room late one night with Cokes and a gallon of strawberry ice cream, with me jumping around and belching and calling out the window like a crazy man: "Shot From Guns! Shot From Guns!" *But then I'll quit: just turn bored or lazy or defiant—it's too long ago now to remember why or what—and go back to the way I was doing things before. And my grades will go back to where they were and stay there; and Rich, after a while of trying not to, will again grow disgusted with me. And a year from now, just as he said, the school will let me go.*

But none of this has happened yet. And as much as I hate these five-thirty mornings, I'm going to miss them terribly when they're gone: the gooey coffee and the slogans, and how it is to feel strong and honest and able when I go to bed at night, and to wake up Shot From Guns.

BY THE SPRING FOLLOWING THE ELECTION, the emails had dwindled. There were only five or six regulars now, and another few occasional voices, most of them still dissecting the November defeat.

"John was too much of a gentleman to engage in the tactics of character assassination," wrote one, a consultant from Washington and one of the first sponsors of our email group. Another argued that it had been John's "patrician aloofness" that had undone him. Arthur—still by far the most prolific among us—felt that he had lacked realness from the start. If he were to seek the presidency a second time, Arthur wrote us all in the early spring 2005: "I would need to see a different candidate, one who is dead-real consistent, courageous, and sincere from the inside out." He then closed with one of his typically grandiose proposals: "Somebody ought to tender all our class discussions to him, and he ought to imbibe them all. It would be an extremely productive use of his time."

No one had heard anything from Rich. I had an email address for him, and had written him the summer before, telling him—honestly—how fondly I remembered that fortnight he'd served as my "personal coach and trainer" and how often over the years, in difficult times, I had thought of him and wished I had a "DeRevere genie" to push me through my days. I was more disappointed than I'd expected to be when I didn't hear anything back.

Others did write back, though. Some of their responses would widen into dialogues, which then sometimes grew farther, into meetings and shared meals. The '58 photo came to me out of one of these, emailed by a classmate in New Hampshire after a long lunch with a second classmate, a wine writer from Sausalito, in the late spring of 2005. Also that spring, I would meet with the old Oklahoma VISTA worker, now a financial planner in New York; and with a wonderfully eccentric inventor and cartoonist, also from New York, who regaled me for two afternoons in his home; and my old dormmate, who'd gone to Vietnam hoping for a final answer to his gayness; and several others.

My early emails to John Kerry, for a long time, went unanswered. Eventually, I did hear back—from his press secretary, who wrote that the senator was too busy to meet but would be happy to answer any questions in writing. The written questions also went unanswered. After a little more than eleven months and forty-odd emails (none of them directly involving John), we would arrange a meeting in Washington.

By the early fall of 2005, I had met with fourteen classmates. John was one of these, as well as four others I would be seeing a great deal of in the year just ahead: Chad Floyd, the Vietnam platoon leader, who would share with me his remembrances of that war and of the country he'd returned to at its end, as well as the battle he was now facing holding together his marriage and his life; Lloyd MacDonald, our class president, now a federal judge in Boston; John Cocroft, also a Vietnam veteran—but with a very different story to tell—who now worked for a soapmaker in Rhode Island; and Philip Heckscher, a New York City artist and teacher, one of the undisputed "brains" of our class, who'd been referred to me in an email by the wine writer. ("I always thought he would end up as an ambassador or running the UN . . . He ended up teaching in NY ghetto schools and living in a gay relationship with some fellow who died of AIDS. I don't know if he's completely out of the closet, so be discreet . . .")

IN OCTOBER CAME THE NEWS OF Rich's death. It arrived as a classmate's email; the attached obituary, from a Florida newspaper, told me that he had died in a hospice in Tallahassee, of cancer, seven months before; that he had a son and a daughter in college, and had been married—to "his wife and best friend"—for thirty-three years. It said that a wake had been scheduled four days after his death at a local pizza restaurant called Barnaby's, "where he has taken his children since they were young."

The eight-line email noted only that Rich had been out of contact with the school since graduating, and had expressed some "less than flattering thoughts" about it to reporters during the '04 campaign. It then closed with this concession to form: "Nonetheless, he was one of us, and it's appropriate that we note his passing."

Rich had never fit. He was short and slight and funny looking, with a head as wide as it was long and ears that stuck out like flattened potatoes. He wore skinny neckties with amusement-park tie clips in the shapes of fish and airplanes. I don't remember him, in all the time of our friendship, being a part of anything. He joined no clubs, had no hobbies that I knew of, and no aptitude whatever for sports. It seemed to me that, for all his warmth and generosity, he had been born without a sense of humor: he seldom smiled publicly, never laughed except out of nervousness or politeness, and studied almost without stop.

He must have been very lonely (his face, as I'm recalling it now, was sadness itself)—as I was also those years. And you'd think, as much time as we spent together, that this might have been something we could have found a way to share. But we never did. The closest we came was when I asked him once—I think one night during the time of his "coaching," when he came to check on me—if he'd ever masturbated. He said that he had, once or twice, but that he hadn't liked the way it left him feeling and he didn't plan to try again.

He was my best friend that year, and probably in all four years I was there. We had almost nothing in common. He was a scholarship student from Illinois, the son of an airline sales manager (though I knew nothing of his family at the time, and never asked); I was a legacied "Paulie" from the Upper East Side of Manhattan, with a stockbroker father, a summer home on a private Adirondack preserve, and a closetful of Brooks Brothers tweeds. Neither of us had many friends, which was probably the biggest reason for our friendship. But he had a kindness about him, too, even before the weeks of his coaching, that showed itself in small ways—a listening ear, unasked-for Milky Ways—and a rawness that touched me somewhere. And privately, I admired him: for his quiet, stubborn sense of purpose, which I couldn't imagine ever achieving and which seemed a kind of purity to me.

We talked about rooming together fifth-form year, but didn't. I don't remember just why. I was probably ashamed of my linkage with him, and fearful of making it formal. For his part, he was fed up by then, I know, with my indifference to schoolwork, which to his mind was the only good reason we were there. However it happened, I roomed alone fifth-form year, as I had all three years before. I don't know if Rich found a roommate or not.

I was gone from the school the year after that—expelled by then, ending any small hope my father still had that I might follow him and my brothers to Yale—and Rich and I would never speak again. I would learn of what happened to him only after he'd died, through the emails of a classmate who recalled it:

In the spring of Rich's sixth-form year, as the writer tells the story, the call had gone out for an emergency replacement for the coxswain of a top intramural crew. It was a coveted assignment, and Rich, with no prior experience but with the physical slightness that is a coxswain's first requirement, had volunteered for the job. He had failed miserably, was cruelly rebuked by the rowers ("If the coxswain fucks up, the oarsmen . . . can be unmerciful"), then released by the coach just prior to Race Day and publicly disgraced.

The emailer, himself an old rower, seemed not to

have gained much distance on the events of those weeks of forty-five years ago. "I expect that Rich suffered," he wrote in one message, and that "the lingering hurt" was probably the cause of his estrangement from the school—because "Crew is a serious business." In a second email, he closed on a note that almost seemed intended to reprise the original hurt:

"He was hopeless, and the oarsmen let him know it. The scars resulting from his short tenure and subsequent removal as coxswain were likely to last a lifetime. RIP."

BEFORE THE WINTER WAS OVER, THE emails would bring the news of two more deaths. In January it would be Walt Ashby, a psychologist from New Jersey, who had frizzy red hair and wore clownish neckties and careless, mismatched clothes—like Rich, he wasn't one of those in thrall of the Regs—and used to make nonstop jokes at the breakfast table when the rest of us were too sleepy and rumpled to do anything but yawn and grunt and ladle out our scrambled eggs. I made a bet with him once, something about the daughter or wife of the teacher—"master"—who presided at our dining-room table that week; I lost, and the price of losing was having to belch or fart in front of the girl or woman the bet had been about. He was like that, goofy and good-natured, given to oddball ideas, one of those few in the class who, without being a jock or a Reg or special or gifted in any particular way, just seemed happy with his own amusements. He didn't carry the same heavy load Rich seemed to; he made a place for himself. His obituary reported that he was "a loving father and made the world's best chocolate chip cookies." My guess is he would have been happy with that.

THE OTHER WAS ARTHUR. THE NEWS came in late November: that he had died two weeks before, alone in his home of a heart attack, probably brought on by the leukemia he'd been fighting for three years. He had mentioned it only once that I know of—in the email that made reference to his "eternal character"—and had never called it by its name.

As with the others, there was an obituary attached. This time with a photo: of a bearded, handsome, half-smiling man, neatly dressed, with dark, thinning hair, who—other than the breadth of his shoulders—looked almost nothing like the Arthur I remembered. The obituary noted that he had "attended St. Paul's School in Concord, N.H." and graduated from the University of Virginia; also that he had "pursued a career in sales" and was "possessed of an active and inquisitive mind." He had never married—but had "given generously of his time and resources" to the Prison Fellowship Ministries and the Christian Blind Association. In lieu of flowers, memorial gifts were to be made to a local Roanoke zoo. (I would have missed the irony if a friend hadn't pointed it out: prisoners, blind people, and caged animals—his sympathies had had a theme.)

The tributes began the same day. Within a week there were more than thirty, some from classmates who had been silent until then; by the time they ended three or four weeks later, there were at least forty, maybe more—eight or ten times the number that the news of Rich or Walt would bring.

It was shame that loosed them. You could see that, plainly. You could read the shame, if you knew the history, on or under the surface of almost any email that was sent.

"I remember visiting [Arthur's] room once during our fourth- or fifth-form year," wrote one classmate, "and being struck by how lonely it felt." "He seemed an anomaly to me," wrote another. "I couldn't understand where he came from, and didn't bother to find out . . . So I do not find it hard to see him as the contrarian, lone (perhaps lonely) abstract thinker he presented in his emails."

One writer recalled a "frigid January day" in 1959 or '60 on the ice at the Lower School Pond, when he had offered a pair of warm gloves to Arthur, who was gloveless: "The gesture, it seemed, meant something to him. He considered me with [new] affection." Another, a boy I wouldn't have thought would have wasted a second's effort on Arthur in those days, told of the time he had "hypnotized" him—at Arthur's request—into talking about his family: "I was moved that this seeming giant would exhibit such earthly sentiments, that he appeared so insecure in his foundations . . . I am saddened by his passing, as well as by the fact that his life appears to have been a rather lonely one."

Several confessed to guilty memories—booby-trapped water buckets, paid-for debasements—including the toilet in the field: "I can bring myself to mention it only in outline," wrote one, a journalist from Connecticut: "a toilet set out in the marsh near the path from the quad to the schoolhouse . . . Arthur on that miserable toilet as we trooped to classes. If someone tried to stop him, I fear he wasn't I."

For a brief period that November and December, the month that followed the news of Arthur's death, the reading of the emails became a daily ritual for me. I looked forward to it. I came to expect, at least once in every new batch, some fresh memory or insight, or new voice, that would set me again to rethinking these strangers I'd known. Some days it would be the purity of a sentiment ("Let us give thanks for [Arthur's] continuing idealism, good spirits and forgiveness."), other times something darker, like the sorrow expressed by several that Arthur had died alone ("I hope others do not have that in their futures, though it is likely to happen to some."). And once in a while would come a memory that would prompt a vision that would set me to laughing out loud—like this account by Geoff Drury, probably Arthur's only real friend at St. Paul's, of how he'd once tried to teach him to break an apple in two:

"He couldn't get the knack of it, and finally, in frustration that his wimpy friend could do something physical that he couldn't, he took the apple in his hands and drove his fingers through it by brute force, smiling grimly as the juice flowed down his forearms and apple fragments littered the floor. He seemed quite satisfied with this technique."

Geoff was one of the new voices. A tall, skinny, bespectacled blond boy, pale and quiet and bookish but often (as I'm recalling him now) enigmatically smiling, he was known by the rest of us mostly for his braininess. I don't remember knowing much about him, except that he was smarter than me. His recounting of the mangled apple was a small part of a much longer letter—a "reminiscence," as he called it—to Arthur's sister Louise, which he was now sharing, with her permission, with the class. It is a strangely sad letter, and sometimes awkward in its candor, though it tries hard not to be:

> [Arthur] and I were both farm boys—the only two farm boys in the school as far as I know . . . [which] made us both obvious outsiders in an environment where the distinction between insider and outsider was all-important, and helped fashion a bond between us that was certainly a comfort for me and, I think, for [Arthur] as well . . .
>
> I have learned more recently that many, if not most, of our classmates saw themselves as outsiders too, on one basis or another, but at that age appearances were everything, and few were willing to share their self-doubts with peers until many years after gradua-

> tion. [Arthur] and I did share them, at least
> with each other, and that made all the
> difference . . .

He hadn't kept up with Arthur in the years since graduation, Geoff confesses toward the close of his letter to Louise. He had tried. He had gotten the same letters and emails others of us had, and had admired in them his old friend's "openness, his passion, his willingness to grapple . . . the courage it must have taken to lay so much of himself out before 70-odd classmates who, when he last had any personal contact with them, were among the most self-centered, cynical, insensitive individuals on the face of the planet." But in the end, he had found Arthur's letters—as we all had—too much:

". . . which made it all too easy to put them aside for later, or to dismiss them, and him, as something one didn't have time to get involved with."

NOT LONG AFTER HER BROTHER'S DEATH in early November, Louise had made a phone call to Lloyd, who had invited her to be a part of our email conversation. Over the next three weeks or so, in an exchange of messages with the class—and in a second, roughly parallel exchange with me—two things became very plain: that she had loved her older brother very dearly, and that she had no idea at all (or pretended that she didn't) of how things had been for him at St. Paul's:

> Dear SPS '62:
>
> Thank you so much for your kind emails and your gracious act of including me in your dialogue . . . Since I have never met any of you, I could only enjoy the St. Paul's portion of [Arthur's] life vicariously. I hope your correspondence with one another will continue; human relationships are of such enormous importance.

The brother who emerges from her letters—first the boy, then the man—is one who seems made for a little sister's love. A big lug from a Pennsylvania farm town, the oldest child of four, desperate for the approval of a distant and difficult father ("an overwhelming personality . . . a terrible temper"), he once, she tells us, as a ten-year-old, changed a flat tire by himself on a highway outside Pittsburgh while she, their mother, and their twin baby brothers waited in the car—"and we all just took for granted that this was a perfectly normal thing." He was smart, he was precocious (sent away to school because "the public schools in our area were so poor"), bigger and stronger than anyone else his age, and he loved football more than anything in life. From his first days at St. Paul's, he brought home stories about his times at fullback with the Isthmian club team ("I was an ardent Isthmian fan, but could only cheer my team to victory after the fact, when [Arthur] came home for vacations."); also about Greek and Latin and *King Lear* and the feats he performed while "hypnotized" by other boys in the class. ("He once came home from vacation with a horrible burn on his wrist," which he explained—"nonchalantly"—was from a candle he had held there while in a hypnotic trance.)

He told her nothing about the toilet in the field, or the enforcement duties, or the "mud crawl" he once did—in the same field, with some of us throwing quarters in his path—or the constant, ever-crueler derision. What he told her was that "he liked the school" and most of the boys he knew there—"despite adolescent cruelty"—and that he had an "increasing appreciation for the opportunities he had."

Much of the rest of what she writes is a eulogy to Arthur. She talks about his love of people and of football, his devotion to prisoners' causes ("He had a huge heart for the underdog, and prisoners were someone he saw as needing wholesome friends."), the medicines he bought for indigent neighbors, the time he'd restrained a house burglar in a headlock, with a wound in his own head that would take sixty stitches to close, while he waited for the police to arrive.

She concludes by seconding a classmate's "wonderful idea" of making our newfound connection a memorial to her brother, then thanks us again for giving her the chance to share her thoughts:

> Over the years I have heard tales about many
> of you, and now I know the names of those

> involved . . . [Arthur] really enjoyed connecting with you, and was very interested in hearing what had become of each of you and what your life experiences had been . . . Your memories have helped me laugh through the tears. It is wonderful to meet you after all these decades.

This is a very sad story. It isn't sad only for how badly Arthur was mistreated, or even because he couldn't or wouldn't see it. It's saddest of all because of how hopeless and inevitable it all seems to have been, because of how badly, how pathetically, all of us, every one of us—every boy in the class who ever tormented him—needed it to happen that way.

"Arthur represented in many ways all of the things we most feared back then," one classmate wrote me in an email the winter of his death. "Isolation, humiliation, scholastic failure, lack of being socially adept. I felt bad for him then but never let him know it. I did have some personal emails with him before he died that let him know how I felt. And he was glad of it. So was I."

We lived in fear, nearly all of us. Fear of failing, of being different, of being stupid, of being hated, of being alone. And along came Arthur: crude, misfitted, socially clumsy, lost in a world he didn't understand—the embodiment of the very worst of our fears. And so we tortured him, we exploited him. From the Regs on down the ladder, but probably no one more than those, like me, who saw ourselves as nearer the bottom than the top. He was our leper, our pariah, our bum in the gutter. He was a gift to us—the same sort of gift a black man is to a racist or a weakling to a bully. And we used him miserably.

And he let us. He crawled through mud and sat on toilets; he made a clown of himself. He told fables to his family about friends he didn't have. Then he forgave us (whatever he may have thought, or once written in a letter, about St. Paul's being an "unChristian place"). He spent a hundred hours the last year of his life writing us mostly ignored emails, at least half of them in reply to messages that hadn't been written to him. He proposed a reunion. He proposed a colloquy on "The Meaning of Integrity." He wrote to apologize for hanging me over the fire escape.

Then he died. And his sister thanked us for the memories. The backwardness of it all is almost beyond belief.

MUCH AS THEY HAD A YEAR earlier after John's election defeat, the emails slowed following the news of the deaths that winter, but never quite stopped altogether. It's hard to say why for sure; I think mostly because of the chance they held out for honesty, so missing among us as schoolmates—and knocked loose now by all that long-ago shame:

"Our emailing has tended to focus on abstract

issues—the Iraq War, the election," a classmate wrote in November in one of the last tributes to Arthur. "[And while] these are important and relevant, I personally think they would be more meaningful . . . if we had a better sense of who we have become—individually, personally, and (somehow) collectively . . . I think what I draw most importantly from listening to [Arthur] is not his substance so much as the fact that he cared to speak to us, personally and poignantly—a worthy model,"

Personal sharing. Arthur as a model. A sense of who we've become. Forty-eight years before, a St. Paul's lower-former, thirteen years old, one day wrote a poem about another, more popular boy. The poem was found and made public. That night or the next, after lights-out in the dorm, four or five boys came to the boy's room and held him down on his bed while they stood over him and slapped his face, one at a time, with their penises (a "cock-whipping," it was called) and made him repeat, until they were done, the lines that they demanded—that only homos write poems to other boys.

There were things you talked about, and things you didn't—at least if you cared, as I did, deeply, about what the Regs would think. And there was a certain way you talked. You talked about sports and you talked about girls. You talked about deb parties in Greenwich or on Long Island, and how many seven-and-sevens you'd had to feed Muffy from Miss Porter's before you got your hand down her front. You talked about summers on Fishers Island or Bermuda, ski trips to Mont Tremblant. You talked, as carelessly as you possibly could, about pink-versus-blue Brooks Brothers broadcloth, Peal's loafers, and Tackleberry skates. You talked about who was a homo, who wasn't a virgin, and who had the best slap shot in the form.

Realness was savaged, an impossible risk. You avoided sharp voice inflections that might give away excitement; you talked with a languor—always—to convey the depth of your indifference to what you were talking about. You never, ever, talked about friendship or fear or loneliness or missing your mother, or how terrified you might be of being hated or alone. If you wanted to show your approval of something, you did it with a shrug or a nod. Sarcasm was the medium: If you were on the wrong end of a skillful "sarc-out" (or "sarc-up") you could walk with your head bowed for two weeks.

There were fewer than a dozen hard-core Regs in our class of a hundred or so. Maybe as few as four or five, and roughly as many pretenders. And there were probably more boys outside their orbit than within it. But whether you were out or in (or trying always, as I was, futilely, to gain access), it was the Regs' presence—their clothes, manners, coolness, their studied disdain (I've never in my life so feared anyone's disdain)—that set the standard, more than anything else, for what happened between and among us at the school.

"Spontaneity, openness, honesty and joy in general are not encouraged. Relationships are often based on one-upsmanship of the most vicious sort. Open frankness is often greeted with cynicism . . . For someone to say to another person, 'I like you,' is almost unthinkable."

We would be gone from the school six years before these words would be written—as part of a three-page, single-spaced notice, challenging every aspect of school life, from academics and mandatory chapel to "moral presuppositions," and signed by more than half the members of the upper two forms. Posted in May 1968 on walls and bulletin boards all over campus, and calling itself the "Manifesto," it would be the beginning of the end of the old way of life at St. Paul's.

BUT NOT YET. WE WERE STILL little pod people in 1961, the year I said good-bye to the school. And memory, as memory does, had frozen us that way. So now, the idea that it might somehow be safe to share ourselves—first glimpsed through our small exchanges of shame—seemed to have come like a boil being lanced. More and more, people were writing now of flubbed marriages, career failures ("I got swindled, hijacked, scared to death . . . all rookie errors, too."), roads not taken, parenting blunders, parents' expectations dashed ("To the end of her days, my mother could never forgive me for choosing the profession I did.").

There was an easiness now, too, to the emails. They were looser, more familiar, sometimes almost mundane—an exchange among rediscovered friends. "Chad, do you still play the drums?" a classmate would write at the end of November; and Chad Floyd, the former Vietnam Marine now an architect in Connecticut, would answer that he did—"now more feverishly than ever"—that he was part of a ten-piece Dixieland band that played on Wednesday nights ("a couple of retired high-school music teachers . . . one guy in his eighties so fat he can no longer play his solos standing up"), and that—now for the benefit of the classmate who'd asked the question about the drums, "who was way better than me at St. Paul's" and will, Chad writes, be surprised to hear it—"I can now even do a few vocals, my best being 'Darktown Strutters' Ball.'"

And the first writer, also a marine officer in Vietnam, now in the New York financial world, will answer back that he, too, still plays some jazz (especially Brubeck), though no longer in a band, that he sings tenor these days in his church choir, and will "never forget our trio, Forbes on bass and you on drums." And this will bring out Forbes, the old bass player, today a Washington lawyer who's been out of touch for years, who will answer with an email that spins off the jazz theme to the chapel hymns of St. Paul's: "that special music, wrapped so tightly around life's solemnities."

And another writer will pick up on that theme ("the thunder of that great organ that I took so much for granted"), then veer off to his remembrance of first hearing Joan Baez, in a dormitory hallway in our third- or fourth-form year: "walking up and down the hall outside a room with a record player, just to hear the song." And so it will go, on and on for weeks.

It's like watching ice break up. It begins at the surface with the first cracks, the first proud or guilty memories entrusted to the group. Then, as the sharing spreads outward and the memories become collective (yes, it really *was* that way, it wasn't only me), there is a ratifying, a kind of expiation. One stranger remembers another, then remembers himself—and nearly always, at such a distance, it is a tender remembering. And the cracking works its way deeper as the old walls and suspicions, now so ancient, are let go.

THE NEWS OF WALT ASHBY'S DEATH, when it came in January, would pass without a lot of remark. We had used ourselves up on Arthur by then—and, to a lesser degree, on Rich—and there wasn't a lot of regret left to go around.

There were ten of us gone now, roughly a tenth of the class. It had begun forty years ago in Vietnam, with Peter Johnson; then there had been a suicide, then nothing for a while; then a plane crash took one, with three or four more scattered over that same decade; then another lull. And now this: three—Rich, Arthur, and Walt—gone in the space of ten months. Looking back at that old third-form class photo, as I'd gotten in the habit of doing with every fresh piece of news, I began to think I saw clusters—two or three near the lower right, another three across the back—like little bites being taken out of the class. But I knew it was only me, trying to put some order to the randomness.

Measuring Up

In the Lower School locker room after supper, a small group of boys have shed their ties and jackets for a game. A bushel of hockey sticks sits in a hamper in the corner; a half-pint milk carton has been flattened for a puck. The goals are two packing boxes, each inside an open locker at opposite ends of the room.

It is September 1957, our first night at the school. I am thirteen, and both excited and very afraid. I don't know any of the boys in the locker room, though I've spent the day with some of them: on the train here from New York, where I watched them talking to each other but couldn't think of anything to say. They are louder now than then, more raucous and confident, thumping the floor with their sticks and calling each other by their newly learned names. Their game has no order, no teams that I can see—just boys shooting and passing, jostling each other, establishing themselves.

It isn't my first time at a boarding school—I've been at one since I was ten—but St. Paul's is my father's school and the school of my uncle and cousins and two older brothers, and I don't remember a time when I didn't know that my father was on the baseball team and my brother was captain of the hockey team and had broken every record in sight. I shed my jacket and take a stick from the hamper, stand a little to one side, and wait. A minute passes. The milk carton goes stick to stick, is shot, passed, deflected, then caroms over to me.

I cradle it, carefully, not wanting to rush, look up for a shot or an open player to pass to—then am slammed, hard, on the shoulder, then shoved, but with more contempt this time than roughness, against a locker door. I stumble. There is a clang. For a second or two, the game stops.

"Beat it, you little shit," *a voice says—or some such words, quick and mean. It belongs to a boy named Peabody, one of those I watched talking and being talked to all afternoon long on the train. Another boy laughs. The milk carton moves on. And I know, with a certainty I am amazed at and will hold in my heart my whole life, that a choosing has taken place and that I have not been picked. I am three hours off the train. It is three months till Christmas. I will remember this moment as my first understanding of despair.*

HIS ENTRY IN THE ALUMNI DIRECTORY told me that he lived in Rhode Island, had a daughter named Sarah (there was no reference to a wife), and worked as a "machine operator" at a soap plant near his home. His father and an uncle were also listed as alumni; both had gone on to Yale, while he had gone instead to a college in upstate New York. From there he'd enlisted in the air force, then been sent to Vietnam (this I'd learned from a classmate who saw him at a reunion) where he'd suffered "some sort of breakdown" but seemed now to be all right.

His name is John Cocroft. I had emailed him for the first time in the summer of 2004, three months before the election. I said I hoped he'd remember me, that we'd been classmates for three years, that I was an author and teacher and was collecting information for a possible book on the class. He wrote back a week later: "I remember you physically in my mind's eye. I'll have to search for anecdotes. I'm willing to do what I can."

Six weeks later he changed his mind: "I have thoughts, but I'm not sure they're worth publicizing. I'd like to stay away for now." I left him alone for five months—until March—then sent him an email with the '58 photo. He wrote back right away:

"I find you in the front in a light-colored jacket with the same screwed-up look that I have on my face. I like the ones who are straightforward and normal looking. The picture is a great study in human development. *Vale,* John."

I didn't know what he meant by any of it—if he meant it to be friendly, funny, or dismissive, or had only grown quirky over the years. (*Vale,* he would remind me later, is Latin for good-bye.) I remembered him well enough: short, blond, well liked, athletic—a hockey player, as were most of us then, but better than most—with an easy smile and a jaunty, jokester's way. In the photo he is half-hidden, scrunched in a back row among taller boys around and behind him, looking not toward the camera but off into the distance as though distracted by something only he can see. He seems lost.

We met finally in April, on a gray weekday morning at an Italian-American pastry place called the Café Roma in the Federal Hill section of Providence. He was there when I arrived, in a flannel shirt and a pair of old work pants, a cup of coffee already in front of him, circling ads with a felt-tipped pen in the Apartments for Rent section of the daily classifieds.

I knew him instantly. He was still compact and solid-seeming, still built like the athlete he'd been, though his hair now was shorter, cut almost to the scalp, and the blond had gone to gray. But it was the smile that gave him away. It is huge and warm and almost impish, and hasn't changed even a tic. His first words to me after I sat down were: "I just got kicked out of my apartment, my life is a total wreck"—but his grin was so wide when he said this I couldn't tell if he was kidding or not.

I would learn soon that he is never kidding when he says things like this, only giving voice to what he's feeling at the moment, which he does with more ease than most of us, and more openness than almost anyone I know. We would meet several times over the next six months or so, all but once at the Café Roma—he liked the coffee, he said, and it was close to where he lived—and each time John would vent himself in the same bursts of self-disclosure. "I never talk to anybody," he said to me the second time we met. "That's the reason you're hearing all this crap."

There had been a problem with a neighbor, he told me—some sort of complaint had been lodged with the landlord in the building where he lived—and now he had six weeks to find a new place. I asked if he thought it might help to talk to the landlord, to explain his side of things. "It wouldn't matter," he answered me. "It's a bad situation. I just need to find another place." He didn't seem deeply troubled by any of this—he may still have been grinning as he told me—but it was plain just the same that the subject had been closed.

It is often this way with him. Exchanges can seem truncated. Subjects open and close like loose boxtops; passions flare, then just as quickly seem to die. It's as though his need for connection were at war with his sense of privacy. Or his feelings were too raw to survive their own expression. Both could be true. There have been some demons. And he has lived a long time alone.

He was divorced in the mid-eighties after a nine-year marriage. He speaks about this with the same chopped, distant certainty with which he discusses his landlord. ("It was a mess . . . we wanted different things . . . she bought me out of the house.") When I ask about his daughter, now in her twenties and teaching school in California, his response is softer—almost tender—but no less abridged: "We email, we talk sometimes by phone. She has her own life. She's doing all right. I haven't seen her in a while." Again, as with the landlord, he plainly has no more to say.

He lives today, as he has for fifteen years, by himself in a one-bedroom apartment in Providence (though no longer, of course, the same one as when we met), drives a '94 Buick Century stacked with old tools and *Wall Street Journals* (money is another subject he shies from, though he does say that his father left him some: "not much, just a few equities, I'm never going to have enough to retire"), and works the three-to-eleven p.m. shift in the packaging room of the Bradford Soap Works in West Warwick, Rhode Island, where he runs the machine that wraps the company's products: Dove, Zest, Pond's, Johnson & Johnson Baby Soap. He's bored by the job, he says, though he's held it fifteen years. When I ask him to describe what exactly he does, he says only that he works on a line with different people on different days: "sort of like when we'd switch off [hockey] lines at St. Paul's." He says, when I ask, that it isn't what he would have planned for his life—"but I try not to think too much about that."

He lives sparely. He walks every morning. He works out three times a week at the Y. He rows a single scull, in warm-weather months, on Narragansett Bay. (He rowed number two on the first Shattuck crew at St. Paul's, placed fifteenth ten years ago in the over-fifty division at the head of the Schuylkill Regatta, then had to quit after bypass surgery but now is rowing again.) He reads avidly, mostly nonfiction: about politics, Antarctica explorations, early Chinese dynasties. He attends seven a.m. Sunday services at the Episcopal church that was once the parish of an ancestor, Thomas Cocroft, a nineteenth-century minister. Sometimes, on summer weekends, he will leave Providence for the cottage in Maine left to him by his parents—wood-heated, on a hillside outside Augusta, with only a single neighbor in view—where he spent his summers as a teen; but the roof is slowly falling in, he says, and he can't afford the repairs. Other times, he will go alone to the beach near his home, often with his old St. Paul's Latin texts, which he enjoys relearning, he says. ("Salve. Tempus Fugit. Vale," was his message to classmates on the Web site of the Hobart College forty-year reunion.) The only person he seems to see much of is his Brazilian girlfriend. They met at the Y three years ago. He has been trying ever since, he says, to find a way to break things off.

Except for his years at school and college and his time in the air force, he has never lived outside Rhode Island. "My roots are here," he explains when I ask about this. Then he pauses, and his voice softens for a second, then hardens again:

"My father was eighty-eight—he died four years ago. My uncle, he was ninety-something, he died around then, too. There's nobody left anymore."

LIKE MOST OF US IN THOSE days, he had come from money, and from what my father liked to call a "good name." Also like a lot of us—it's the oldest story in the world—the money was mostly gone by the time the legacy got around to him (he isn't even sure who paid the tuition bills for St. Paul's) and the name was pretty well faded. But there had been a time.

John's great-grandfather, Arthur Hamilton Watson (John's middle name is Watson), a descendant of Roger Williams and the only child of an Episcopal minister—there are ministers on both sides—was graduated from Brown University in Providence in the class of 1870, took a job the following year as a clerk in a wholesale shoe firm—Green, Anthony and Co. of Providence—and by the time of his death forty years later was president of the Providence, Fall River and Newport Steamboat Company, vice president of the Narragansett Electric Company, and director or past director of half a dozen more Rhode Island banks and firms. His wife, Anne Potter Sprague, whom he married in 1873, was descended from two Rhode Island governors. One of them had founded the Cranston Print Works, earlier known as the Sprague

Print Works, among the largest textile mills in the country at the time.

But six months after the wedding came the banking panic of 1873, and the five-year depression that followed. The mill failed; the Sprague fortune dwindled, then was divided, then redivided, among heirs. "The money spread out" is how John puts it. "There wasn't much left by the time our turn came around. My parents, my family in general—we were more background than bank account by then."

But background matters deeply in such families—often at the expense of other things—and appearances, when possible, are kept up. John's father, by whatever means, was sent off to boarding school at eleven or twelve years old (to Fay School in Massachusetts, where I would be sent myself years later), and from there, probably as a third-former—ninth-grader—to St. Paul's. Then to Yale. For John, as for me and untold others over at least four generations, it was understood early that the path was to be the same: "I was a Yale guy," he says. "It was a bred-in kind of thing. St. Paul's was the way in the door."

He entered in the fall of 1958, a year after I did, as a member of the third form. He was fourteen, he says, and "scared to death." When I ask him about this, the answer he gives is my first real clue to why he keeps, in so many ways, such a distance from the world:

"Everyone was so *smart*. Phil Heckscher, Steve Fields, Max King—all those guys with the big brains. All my life I'd been around people pretty much like myself, and now all of a sudden I'm surrounded by all these guys so much smarter than me. And they all made it look so easy. *So easy*. That's the part that used to get to me the most."

We talk for a while about the class brains, naming names, drawing distinctions between the math-genius eggheads and those who, we both agree, were "all-around smart." At some point during this, John starts to silently chuckle, then to laugh. I have no idea why, though I've learned by now not to be surprised by anything that happens with him. So I wait. The laughter eases gradually back to a chuckle, and from there to a slow rolling of his head, which continues on and off through most of what follows—John's reprisal of his first night at St. Paul's:

"There we all are in Brewster [the third-form dormitory], sitting around in somebody's room—me, Max King, Malcolm Smith, a bunch of other guys—nobody knows anybody else, everybody's nervous, trying to make an impression, all that kind of cool-guy, rah-rah stuff . . .

"And I'm starting to think that things are going to be okay. I mean, I'm liking these guys pretty well, and they all seem like they're getting along with me. And then the bell rings for supper, and we all head off toward the Upper [which houses the student dining hall, a five-minute walk from the dorms], still together, kind of talking as we go . . .

"And then all of a sudden one of them looks at me and points, and says, 'Hey, Cocroft, you forgot your necktie'—and I look down and it's true. So I turn around and start running back to Brewster to get my tie. And by the time I do that, and I get to the Upper, everybody's sitting down already and the meal's started and I can't find any of the guys I was with . . .

"So that's how it began. I've been there five or six hours, and already I'm out of step—they're going one way on their way to have supper together, and I'm running the other way to get this necktie I forgot. Then, a week later, I got a forty on my first math test. I feel like, between the two of them, that was a metaphor for my whole time at St. Paul's."

He is smiling as he tells this, but there is pain in his voice. And there would be. It's a painful story to hear. I think for a moment about sharing with him my own first-night story—about the locker-room hockey game—then decide not to, and we move on. But I have a sense of what that necktie must have cost.

I never would have guessed it, though. Not of John. I wouldn't have thought he'd had an anxious moment in his four years at St. Paul's. I hadn't know him well—we were on different clubs, played different sports (except for hockey, which almost everybody played), and were never in the same dorm—but there'd been an easiness about him you couldn't help but pick up. And a warmth, and sense of safety, that could be hard to find with other boys. He had seemed real to me. Not like the Regs or their imitators, the clench-jawed, barb-tongued, Brooks Brothers mannequins—boys in drag as little men—who had seemed at times to rule the school. He could be a clown at times, but that was more refreshing than foolish: there weren't many among us, in that wary little world, who would willingly draw the laughter on themselves.

Everyone had liked him. As I picture him today, he is walking in a crowd, jostling, sleepy-eyed, a little disheveled, and always with that grin. And he was a jock—football, hockey, and crew—and, by his senior year at least, a joiner: chapel warden, dorm supervisor, and member of the Missionary Society. I'd never have guessed his troubles. I probably envied him.

I tell him this. He laughs. He drums his fingers a couple of times on the table, then does his version of a mock-dramatic pause:

"I borrowed their brains." He says it a second time, with only a little less inflection: "I borrowed their brains. I figured out, when I hung around them long enough, it felt like I got smarter, like their brains rubbed off on me. And I'd start talking like them, and acting the way they did. I had to work hard to get it right, though, to get that—you know, that cool, casual, 'Oh, this is nothing' way of being they all had."

The longer we talk, the fuller and sharper the memories become, the more he seems to warm. At one point I realize we've been sitting at our little table for three hours with only a single refill of coffee and a muffin each. The tables around us start filling—it is the lunch crowd now, mostly secretaries and swarthy young men in sweatshirts—and John, whose voice has risen and quickened as his involvement has picked up, seems heedless of all of it. He talks about hockey, rowing, dorm life, his roommates, the study-hall fire fifth-form year, his troubles with Latin and math. He talks about the club football team he played on with Arthur, on which John had been captain and Arthur had been fullback—and the terror of every opponent—and how he'd gotten an email from him the year before, not long before he died, saying that he thought he should have been captain instead:

"I wrote him back and said I agreed, that I totally agreed. It's forty-some years later and he wants to be captain—what am I going to do, tell him no?"

He calls up things I haven't thought of in decades. The school store, run by a crusty, cigar-smoking curmudgeon named Art King, a legend even before we arrived, who would make you love his insults while he taped your hockey sticks. The Regs, and the ridiculous, clench-throated shibboleth they shared among themselves—"*BAAA-DOOH!*" is how John recaptures it, complete with a face-shriveling sneer that actually seems almost right. The '62 hockey team, the worst in a decade ("but we always lost by small margins"), on which he played with John Kerry, Bob Mueller, and five or six others in the class. The names of sixty years of Ferguson Scholars, hand-inscribed on oak plaques, lost the night the study hall burned down. (Says John: "They were the heart and soul of the school.") And the longer he talks and the later it gets, the more I come to understand: he *loved* the school, he honestly loved it. He still does.

He talks about the fire in personal terms, and as though it happened last year: the frostbite he suffered to his toes trying, he says, to help the firemen; his belief about who was responsible (it was thought to be arson, though no one was ever named); the misery of watching "that awful, all-night waste." He recounts, one by one with undisguised reverence, a litany of the school's rituals and traditions: its sports clubs, rowing clubs, Honor Code, school prayer, special holidays, the Sunday-night evensong service.

At first I just listen. But then, more and more as his memories string together, I begin to remember, too, and to put in my own versions and additions. At one point, we go on for several minutes, interrupting and overlapping each other like schoolkids, about the annual surprise "Turkey Holiday," announced every November on the day—or *around* the day, you could never be sure exactly and that was most of the thrill—that the ice on Turkey Pond turned black and skateable with the first hard winter freeze. You would never know for sure till morning chapel, and only then with the reading by the rector of a certain verse from Zechariah ("And the streets shall be full of boys and girls playing in the streets of Jerusalem . . ."). Five hundred breaths would be intaken as one—literally—as the rector reached the word "boys." It's a sound I can almost still hear.

I loved some of those small rituals, maybe almost as much as John did. I loved their sureness, their oldness; I loved their elegant beauty. I wasn't too young to be stirred by the sweet plainness of the school prayer, which

I've never forgotten, and always recite when I'm asked somewhere to contribute a grace to a meal. (It was years before it occurred to me that the message of its words was not one we often saw backed by example.)

Grant, oh Lord, that in all the joys of life
We may never forget to be kind.
Help us to be unselfish in friendship,
Thoughtful of those less happy than ourselves,
And eager to bear the burdens of others.
Through Jesus Christ, our Lord.
Amen.

JOHN AND I TALK FOR A while, our first morning especially, about the unfulfilled Yale birthright we share. I tell him the blow it was for my father. He says he thinks his father accepted it well enough, that it was more of a blow for him: "I remember the first time it got hinted at," he tells me, by some St. Paul's master, that he might not make it there—"and I'm thinking, *'What's he telling me? What's he telling me? Is he telling me I don't measure up? That I'm not an Ivy Leaguer?'*"

I hear these words, and some of the others John falls back on sometimes when he's in his old-school mode of thinking—a Yale man, an Ivy Leaguer, "measuring up," "a bred-in kind of thing"—and it's like listening again to my father, who's been dead now more than forty years. He swore by these same abstractions, called them by the very same names—mostly, in his case, because there was so little else to swear by. And it used to scare me when he'd say them, because I'd know that the reminders of my failure were never far behind.

John's father, though, from what he tells me, was not such a man as my father. He didn't talk about legacies or good names, or place weighty expectations on his son. "He would have liked for me to go to Yale," John tells me. "I probably always knew that. But he didn't make an issue of it. There was no big pressure. He was a good father. They were both good. They were good parents to my sisters and me."

Still, Watty Cocroft had gone to St. Paul's and to Yale, as had his older brother. And it may have been their mother, John's grandmother, of the Watson-Sprague lineage ("an elegant, refined lady who cared about good things"), who took care of those tuition bills. So the pressures were probably there. But subtle and unspoken, more like something in the water or air.

Whatever their source, it is clear he feels their weight. He speaks often, with unconcealed pride, of his family's early history: the Episcopal ministers, the governors, his grandfather the architect, his great-grandfather the "textile king." His memories of the past seem almost reverential—which may be why he seems, in so many ways, to relive them. "It's like muscle memory," he says when I ask about this. "It's just ingrained in me." But the way he laughs when he says this tells me he knows it's not much of an answer.

And if there was some single defining moment, some turn in the road on which other turns and choices would depend, it may have been the day when—as he tells it—the man in the Yale admissions office told him (as Yale admissions people, in those chummier, clubbier days, must sometimes have said to alumni sons): "You can come to Yale if you want to, but we think you'd be happier somewhere else." Or, as John transcribes it in the retelling: "You can come to our party if you have to, but we really don't want you there."

So instead he went to Hobart, in upstate New York, where he would spend the next four years, he says, "comparing every classroom and building column to the way things were at Yale." He majored in history because "it was a whole lot easier than math," dated a woman who threw him over for a dental student from Dartmouth, and finished, he tells me, at the dead bottom of his class.

Midway through his senior year—late 1965, with Vietnam climbing the headlines and draft call-ups already at forty thousand a month—the college was visited by a recruiter from Navy OCS. The war was still young. The lies, and the body bags, wouldn't be leading the six o'clock news for another year or more.

"It was a good war as far as I was concerned," John says to me. "I never questioned it. Why would I question it? I was still buying into that whole World War II–generation thing, my father's generation thing—you know, America the liberator, America doing good in the world. I figured I'd be part of something noble and historic . . . I was twenty-one or something. I didn't know anything about anything, I didn't know what I wanted to do with my life. I guess I probably thought that flying a jet off the deck of an aircraft carrier might be a pretty cool thing to do."

And there was a second factor, he says, more personal, and maybe the bigger of the two: "My father [after Yale] had been a navy commander. I hadn't made it to Yale. I figured maybe I could at least do the navy part of the thing."

At some point during the screening interview, the recruiter, noting that John was a hockey player, asked him a question: What would he do, in the final minutes of a close game, if he found himself with the puck and a clear shot at the opponent's goal—but with a teammate, also open, alongside him? Would he shoot or would he pass?

"What I'd probably do is shoot," John says to me. "But passing is the *Christian* thing—that's what I learned at St. Paul's, and I'm thinking maybe that's what the guy wants to hear. So I say to him, 'I'd pass.'

"'That's the *wrong answer,* John,' the guy says. 'When a navy flier has a shot, he takes the shot.' And I knew right there I wouldn't be flying for the navy."

THINGS HAPPENED FAST IN THE FOUR years that followed. "They're kind of a blur," John tells me. And as he tries his best, over two mornings, to recount them, it's plain to see that they are.

He graduated in June 1966. By September he was in the air force in Texas—he'd been drafted after graduation, then decided instead to enlist—awaiting tech school as a mechanic. They sent him to Panama, where he worked for eighteen months refueling planes. It was dull work. There was a lot of drinking. Then they sent him to Vietnam.

It was the spring of 1968 by then, the spring of the Tet Offensive. No one was believing the generals anymore. U.S dead had passed thirty thousand. They were marching in the cities now—New York, Washington, London, Chicago—closing down campuses, announcing weekly body counts every Thursday on TV. It was a very different war.

But for John, refueling helicopters in Vung Tau on the South China Sea, listening to the stories the fliers told coming in from their missions or being medevacked in on litters with their wounds, sitting at bars every night with soldiers or airmen just back from Khe Sanh or Qui Nhon (where Peter Johnson had just died), it was still the same war it had been:

"I'm there, I'm looking at all these planes and tanks, all this power, and I'm thinking, 'I'm a part of this—I'm a *part* of this—and this is a great thing we're doing here, we're giving these people back their country, this is great, this is really, really great.' It's all that chauvinist stuff, the same stuff my father was part of in the war—you know, all that wave-the-flag, shoot-the-guns, support-the-home-team stuff. So I'm looking at all those folks around me, and I'm thinking, *'Yeah, I can get on this train . . .'* "

Then one day, probably in the late summer or early fall of 1968, he was sitting around in his barracks, he says, drinking tequila and reading an old issue of *Time*. The story was about Clark Clifford, who'd replaced Robert McNamara as defense secretary earlier that year and had just turned, unexpectedly (as McNamara had before him), against the war.

Something happened to John when he read this. It's hard to know what a psychologist would say about it, but it sounds, to hear him tell it, as though all those years of striving and joining, of borrowing brains and following in footsteps, all came unglued at once.

"I was a believer. Ready to do my duty, ready to goose-step like some Nazi if that's what they wanted from me. Then I read the article. And what's he saying? He's saying, *'Whoa, hey, this is all wrong here—Lyndon, we gotta get the fuck outta Vietnam.'* It's like somebody taps you on the shoulder and says, 'Hey, no, this is all a big mistake, forget everything we told you, we gotta reverse this, we gotta turn this car around.'

"Well, I *couldn't* turn it around. I just couldn't. And I flipped."

Exactly what happened is unclear in the telling. He was drunk at the time, he says, and the events of that day and the few that followed are muddled in his head. He knows he got up on some sandbags with a crowd of airmen around, and that he lost himself. *"We're all just fuckin' sheep!"* he shouted at them. *"This whole war is just a goddamn show—we're the only ones who don't know it! We're just a bunch of sheep, is what we are!"*

Then he put his hand through a door. His wrist was broken. They sent him to a medical unit ("I'm lying there next to these guys who are missing their legs—I felt like a piece of scum."), then to Cam Ranh Bay to see a shrink, who asked him, he remembers, "How do you like your mother?" Then they sent him to a hospital in Japan. ("They said it was to fix my wrist, but what they *really* were trying to do was dry me out.") He left the hospital, got into a bottle of 151-proof rum, and blacked out.

They sent him home, to Westover Air Force Base in Massachusetts, where they had him see more shrinks. ("I felt like a war victim—but I *wasn't*. Not that kind anyway. I was so ashamed.") Then they sent him to Okinawa to refuel B-52s. There was a card game. He got into a fight. Something—a brick maybe—came through a window and hit him on the head. He blacked out—it would take fifty-two stitches to close up his head. They sewed him up, then sent him back to Massachusetts. In the fall of 1970 they released him. He was still "screwed up on booze," he says—"really bad"—and full of anger. But it was probably nothing an air force shrink was going to fix.

"I had this kind of effete view of the war. Duty, honor, all that Ernie Pyle sort of stuff. I was keeping this journal, writing down all these 'good-guy-bad-guy, war-is-hell' kinds of thoughts . . .

"Then I saw the real shit. There was *no* honor, they didn't know what they were doing over there. I couldn't be part of it anymore. I couldn't be part of their war. I had a turning-away."

He came home to Rhode Island. Everything had changed. Jane Fonda was speaking on college campuses; there had been bank bombings in Berkeley, a hundred thousand marchers in Washington, four dead in April at Kent State. The following spring, two hundred thousand veterans would march on the Capitol in protest against the war. A thousand of them, including John Kerry, who would testify before Congress the same week, would throw their medals over the Capitol fence.

John's mother was among those whose sympathies had shifted. "She'd completely come around," he says. "She was practically ready to march." She gave him an anti-war button. He was moved, even tempted. But he couldn't put it on.

"It just wasn't that easy. I was still angry, I still felt totally betrayed. But I couldn't do that. I couldn't be with those guys. I couldn't just say, 'Hey, yeah, fuck the war, let's go smoke a joint, make some noise, go march on the Capitol.' For me, it was more complicated than that."

IT'S AMAZING SOMETIMES HOW A PERSON can change without changing, can hold on to all the old tics and habits, all the old identifying marks, while the mix underneath is seething or hardening as life burrows deeper toward the core.

It seems this way with John. Sitting across from him these mornings at the Café Roma listening to his remembrances, it is still easy to see—even through the anger that seizes him at times—the boy inside the man. Part of it is the smile, which expands across his face in just the same way as his blue eyes narrow and brighten. And the way he has of peering so intently when he talks, as though he could hold you in place with his look. And his clownish way of parodying others—or just as often, himself. I wouldn't have been able to depict any of this, or even to know that I knew it; but seeing it again is like hearing an old tune I'd forgotten, or catching the trace of something familiar in a creaking door or a smell.

But it's a different feeling now. It's a different message. From his opening, grinning line to me—"My life is a total wreck"—the laughter now has an edge to it it couldn't have had at sixteen. He makes jokes about being slow-witted (which he's nowhere close to being), tells brittle, oddly funny anecdotes about his problems with alcohol and his year in Vietnam; shares a story about his bust-out as a salesman and another about being fired from a job at an insurance company, years ago, for doing crossword puzzles on company time.

There have been a lot of jobs. A job in sales, another with a yarn maker, two jobs in insurance, a job in the late seventies constructing solar homes. ("I was going to be a solar-home king . . . Five dollars an hour plus Blue Cross—'Bring those two-by-fours over here, John.'") There was a carpenter's job, a job with a boat builder, a job refueling planes on an air base in Massachusetts, a four-year job in the weave room of a textile plant. ("Fifteen looms, very loud, very definite—SLAM!-BANG!-WHAM!—just like my brain.") But nothing worked out for long. One time he fell asleep at his desk in the office, another time it was the crossword puzzles; the commute was too long for one of the insurance jobs. In 1980, during his time as a carpenter, he threw his back out and was out of work for two years.

That was when he stopped drinking. He was still married at the time; their daughter was a baby. When his back improved enough, he built a home for the three of them. Then he went back to work, this time with the boat builder. In 1986, for reasons he won't go into ("It was too big a mess to even begin to describe"), his marriage collapsed and his wife threw him out of the house. For a time—several weeks, a month or more, he isn't exactly sure—he lived in a tent in a campground in Middletown, Rhode Island.

All this he tells me easily, almost blithely, grinning here and there, sometimes laughing at the jokes he tells on himself. It is an edgy laughter, but not enough to make me uncomfortable or to stop me from laughing with him, which I do. "I have a hard time with success," he says at one point. "I'm not good at success." This leads him into a cataloguing of what he sees as his defining failures: Hobart versus Yale, fueling planes in Vietnam instead of flying them, an early setback as a sales trainee at Bradford Soap Works, the same company he runs a machine for today.

"I don't like expectations," he says then. "Family, work, women, whatever—I hate it when they keep expecting things of you."

EXPECTATIONS. IT WAS EXPECTATIONS that began all this, that began everything. St. Paul's was an expectations *mill*—especially for boys, like John, with industry barons for grandfathers and fathers or uncles who'd laid down the path to Princeton or to Yale. For most of these boys, the legacy worked as it was meant to: they grew up with their sights on life as grooved as their table manners. They may have anguished over failing, or even sometimes failed, but they rarely jumped the track.

For others, the effect was different. For a few, it was almost cruel.

"I feel like St. Paul's, it gave me this sort of superego, you know what I mean?" John says to me toward the end of one of our days. "But what it wants me to be, what it showed me is out there, is just too painful to live with, too hard to even try. I feel like, if I were a politician I'd say the wrong thing. If I were a surgeon I'd probably slip on the knife. I'm just a spaz with life."

He's grinning as he says this. He's talking about pain and failure, and his eyes are as hard as his meaning, but he's grinning by the end. Then he finishes, with his joke about being a "spaz"—an everyday St. Paul's derision in those days—and breaks into a laugh.

It's hard to know how long it's been this way with him, how long ago he quit trying and became his own best joke. It may have begun as early as St. Paul's, but not in any way you would have noticed. He was still trying then—and succeeding, by any measure the rest of us would have known. And he was trying four years later when he saw that navy recruiter. Even pumping fuel in Vietnam, to hear him tell it, he was trying his best to be a part of things. Then came that story in *Time*—that may have been the start of the hardening, of the slow retreat from the world. Whether it was or not, the message he took from it seems to have attached itself to more than just his belief in his country or the war:

"They tell you, 'Work hard, keep your nose clean, do the right thing, and you'll end up in the right place at the end.' Then you find out it's all a big lie. The war, the rah-rah, all of it, a big lie. You find out your enemy—he's not always just the guy on the other side of the wire . . .

"I couldn't handle that. I couldn't handle the backwardness. It's like somebody tells you there's no such thing as truth."

So he came home confused and angry, too confused maybe even to give his anger a name, as others, like John Kerry, were doing by that time. And he kept on drinking and began going through jobs—he was only twenty-six, there would always be another job. And there *was* another, then another and another, then a marriage and a daughter, and more jobs. And somewhere along the line, not so much by decision as slow, incremental default, he just began to realize that he didn't want to play the game. ("It can all start with a simple act, a simple answer, like what I told that navy guy that day. Then you wake up one morning and you've taken this big direction with your life.") There's no knowing what he told himself: maybe that he wasn't smart enough or tough enough to win it, or that he was just too tired of what it took—the brain-borrowing, the effortless cool, always saying the Christian thing. Or maybe it was because of Vietnam. Or all of it together. Whatever it was, the sense you get is that John over time just decided, consciously or not, to throw away the script.

And he has at least half-succeeded. There is no defeat about him. He never once blames life, bad luck, or anyone else for his troubles. He's a cheerful slogger. And honest, or as honest as he can let himself be. I have liked him from the moment we shook hands.

ONE OF THE LAST TIMES WE saw each other, on an April afternoon at a little lunch place across from the Amtrak station in Providence where he'd just met my train, I asked him the question: how do you feel about life?

He gave his big grin across the table. Then he said, flatly, but without the grin coming loose: *"I feel like impending doom."* Still the grin. But he meant it. I could see that he meant it. He began nodding his head slowly, a little solemnly, as though to make sure I understood—this was not a trifling thing he had said.

I cracked up. I laughed and I laughed; I couldn't stop laughing. If I'd had anything in my mouth at the time, I'm sure I would have spit it out. John looked confused for a second, then began laughing himself. So there we sat, the two of us at this little table in the corner, for probably a full minute, laughing our heads off like a pair of old fools, neither one of us knowing quite why.

That's the beauty of John. And the oddity. He can tell you he hates his life in such a way as to cause you to understand—all at the same time—that he does indeed hate it, that he probably isn't going to do anything to change it, that this is a truly sad state of affairs for him, but that you really needn't worry except maybe for five minutes. Because *he* won't. Then, with that ground covered, you can move on to other, more prosaic things. Like his lousy job, or his heart condition, or the Brazilian girlfriend he can't seem to say good-bye to.

So, I ask him now, if you could do anything at all, have anything you wanted, what would it be? Would you want to be president of the company? Would you want to be a banker or a lawyer or an architect, or what?

He thinks a minute, looks around the room, then he does that big grin one more time.

"Let's say I make a hundred dollars a day. And the top guy, let's say he makes five thousand. Well, I could move my car out of my garage, borrow a lot of money, and buy a whole big load of machinery, then move that into my garage and start manufacturing stuff. And before long, maybe I'd be the one making the five thousand dollars . . .

"But no, thanks. Never mind. Just give me my hundred dollars. Let me go home when my time's done. Let me go home and row my boat."

IT'S NEVER THAT SIMPLE, OF COURSE. You can never throw all those scripts away, not in any way that leaves you clean. And John hasn't. And he knows that he hasn't. That's why he rails against expectations. That's why, so often, there is such an edge to his jokes.

Most of the time he lives with it, just as we all do with the demons and entrapments we create for ourselves. He rows his boat, reads his Latin books on the beach, is happy with his hundred dollars. He keeps the past close by—often so close it tortures him—but mostly out of sight.

Then there are the times, no doubt more than he would admit to me, for all his openness, when it catches up with him. One of them may have been the 2004 election.

"I played hockey with John Kerry, I lived with the guy for four years. And then he goes and does *that*—he runs for the presidency and almost wins. He was *almost president*. I had to look at myself. So where am I? What am I doing? Why am I where I am?"

I tell l him I think John's candidacy raised those same questions for a lot of us. I don't know if he believes me, but he doesn't seem consoled.

Chapel Mornings

I love this place. It is my favorite place in the school. I love how dark it is, how somber and silent—there is a silence here even when there is noise, even when the organ is playing and every voice is raised—and how full of shadows no matter what time of day. I like to look at the scenes in the stained-glass windows of the saints and disciples and their horses, and how they move in the light when I raise and lower my head. I like the way the wood feels under my fingers, old and smooth and rubbed by so many hands. I feel protected here.

I have felt this way since the first morning as a second-former, the start of my first full day at the school. I had hardly slept the night before—the boy in the next alcove had been crying. I whispered something, meaning to be friendly; he whispered back, "Fuck you." An hour or so later they came and took him to the infirmary. Then they must have called his parents. We would never see him again.

Some of us thought the rector might say something, that first morning in chapel, about the missing boy. But he didn't. He just waited till his time came in the service, got up from where he sat in the back, and looked out at us, very directly—the new boys, in the front rows of pews with the upperclassmen and faculty behind—and said, in this sort of strong, kind, fatherly voice, that he wanted to welcome us into the St. Paul's Family, that he knew there were some among us who might be feeling lost or alone that morning but that we would be amazed how quickly the days and months would pass, that soon we would be sitting in the back pews ourselves and then be outside on the lawn in our caps and gowns with our diplomas on our way to yet another new beginning. I believed him—and felt, as I listened, that he was talking only to me.

Then, as he finished, or not long after, there came this sudden, huge, single chord from the organ—it seemed to carry by vibration, from the altar and chancel, off the high stone arches and sidewalls, the length and width of the nave. And as it ended, a second chord; and with this the voices of the choir, followed by the rest of us—the new boys still awed and befuddled, our heads bent to our hymnbooks, the old boys singing by heart—five or six hundred voices in all:

Fight the good fight, with all thy might,
Christ is thy strength and Christ thy right,
Lay hold on life, and it shall be
Thy joy and crown eternally

Run the straight race through God's good grace,
Lift up thine eyes and seek his face
Life with its way before us lies,
Christ is the path and Christ the prize

This was wonderful to me. The majesty of it, and the manliness—the good fight, the straight race, the path, the crown, the prize—coming on top of the kindness and comfort of the rector's words, found some place inside me, filled some hole, that I hadn't known was there.

But it isn't only that. It isn't only the comfort and the grandeur. There is mystery here, too—you can feel it. It used to frighten me a little, those first months of second-form year, when I would come by myself when the chapel was empty, to practice with the choir in the choir room in the back: the long nave and high, vaulted arches that can cause even the smallest sounds to echo like ghosts; the white marble statue of a naked soldier collapsing into the arms of the wide-winged angel of death. It all seemed ancient and forbidding, and somber, like death itself.

But by third-form year I stopped being afraid. And

sometimes even, at the end of practice, I would walk out through the nave instead of by the choir-room door, just to read the statues and plaques to all the dead alumni and listen to the echoes of myself.

ONE OF THE FIRST EMAILS I wrote, a month before the 2004 election, was to Lloyd. He had been our president; it seemed a natural starting point. Other than this, though, and his unflappable sureness (what John Cocroft would have called his "'Oh, this is nothing' way of being") and a particular kindness he had once extended to me, I remembered almost nothing about him. In that opening email, I addressed him by the wrong name.

He wrote back within days, corrected me graciously, and said that he'd be happy to talk. He said that St. Paul's had been on his mind lately, partly because of the election coming up—and "all the (deserved) attention to John"—but also because, in cleaning out the attic of his mother's house (she had died the previous year), he had come across some of his old letters from St. Paul's: "None of any but personal interest, but they did time-warp me back 40 years."

It was five months before our next contact, though I would read, in the meantime, several of his emails to the class. One of these, written from his law office in Boston shortly before midnight on a Tuesday two weeks before the election, seemed to suggest that he wasn't a Kerry fan ("I fear John is being sucked into what is essentially an appeasement mode.")—but also that he still carried with him an affection for the school, and for his years there, that I could only marvel at:

"It just struck me that writing to all you guys, after the span of 42 years and all the indelible memories I have of every one of you on the 'To' list of this 'Reply to All' email, is probably the only thing right now that could give me more pleasure than having gone home and watched the Red Sox take another step in overcoming The Curse."

We met for the first time the following April, at the Harvard Club in Boston (Lloyd is a Harvard alumnus), five months after the Kerry defeat. When I first saw him again, he was hanging up his trenchcoat in the coatroom between the elevator and the French-doored entrance to the bar. He was bald, as he'd been on his way to being at seventeen, but thinner now than I remembered, and not as tall (about my height—I'd recalled him as towering over me). He was tanned for April, and looked very fit, and was wearing a dark blue suit. I knew him first by his eyes, which are very soft and direct; after that his voice—calm, almost lulling—and then his smile. When we shook hands and said our greetings, I could see that the sureness was still there.

We got a table by the window—thirty-eight floors up, with a view of Back Bay and the harbor—where he bought me several ginger ales and we talked for two hours, sketchily and almost at random, about how things had been with each other and with this or that member of the class. He had gone from Harvard on to law school; had been a prosecutor in the U.S. attorney's office, then in private practice until a month or two before, when he'd been appointed a judge. He'd been married for twenty years, divorced, and remarried ("It's way too long a story."), had two grown kids. And how about me? I told him I'd had a checkered time for a while, had bounced around colleges, had also been married and divorced—though never remarried—that I had a son in his late twenties, had worked for a newspaper, written for magazines, that the book I was starting on now—about our class—would be my fourth.

I told him nothing about the troubles I'd had during college—what all that bouncing had been about—or in the years just after, or how lost I had felt at St. Paul's. As it turned out, I could have; we might have found our commonness far sooner than we did. But there was no way to know that at the time.

He seemed happy to be there—although careful, a little sparing, with his words. He seemed much as I'd have expected him to be. ("Still the president," I would write later in the notes I took of the meeting, and "the perfect judge.") I asked him how he thought he'd come to be our president. He laughed and answered quickly, as though he'd been asked the question before: "I think I just managed not to make any enemies." I said I thought that was a pretty good trick at St. Paul's.

WE HAD BARELY KNOWN EACH OTHER. He had played football, was straitlaced, well liked, hardworking, and had always seemed to me (like several others in the form) to exist somehow on a higher, less accessible plain. He was tall and bulky and looked older than his age, one of those who, as early as fourteen, was probably already shaving. I was short and as skinny as a stick, looked a year or two younger than I was, and never got past peach fuzz until my last half-year at St. Paul's. These differences alone, in that close, combative little world, were enough to divide us like islands.

He was quiet, though it never seemed out of shyness. There was a calm about him, a sort of kindly aloofness, that seemed to come from somewhere more real, less studied, than the attitudes of other boys. Probably not many among us would have named him as our first choice for president, but once his name was out there, it was hard to imagine anyone else so natural for the job: coolheaded, decent, fair-minded, a reassuring hand at the wheel. Every senior class should have its Lloyd.

The only place our paths ever crossed was on the track. We were both sprinters, and both members, our fifth-form year—my last one at the school—of the four-man, 440-yard relay. I don't remember all the details that led up to Lloyd's kindness to me. What I remember is that I'd had troubles during practice, more than once, with the baton handoff, and every member of the team knew it; and that one day, at an interschool meet about halfway through the season, with a two- or three-step lead heading into the box, I had botched the handoff again—the baton was dropped, the race was lost, and (as I remember it) the whole meet as a result.

It would be hard to overstate the miseries this cost me—not so different, probably, from Rich's tribulations sixth-form year after flubbing as coxwain on the crew. I was shunned. Then I was mocked. A week later, boys were still passing me in the hallways making jerky, spastic-looking movements with their hands. I wanted to be dead. I tried to quit the team, but the coach wouldn't hear of it. "Character grows from failure," he told me, or words to that effect—and swore I would thank him one day.

One afternoon just before practice, Lloyd approached me on the track. He asked if I wanted to try some passes: "After practice, just you and me, see if we can smooth things out. We need you on the team."

And we did. Very quietly, for several days or a week, twenty or twenty-five minutes every day, until I could pass the stick with my eyes closed. And no one dared say anything because it was Lloyd. I never dropped the stick again; we won some big meets that year. And when I tried to thank him, he just kind of shrugged and said it would have been a shame to lose me from the team.

An hour or so into our meetings I would remind him of his kindness. He said he could only barely recall it, which didn't surprise me at all. To him it must have seemed a simple enough gesture. I couldn't name three others to match it in my four years at St. Paul's.

IT WAS AN ODD EVENING. ON the surface, very warm and collegial, with some real honesties imparted, no awkwardness you could have put your finger on, and at least one or two exchanges that seemed to cut very naturally through the years. We talked about our kids, our jobs, our little ailments. We traded remembrances: a teacher, the track coach, the night the study hall burned down—his loyalties to the school seemed rooted very deep. An hour passed, then most of another. Neither of us seemed in a hurry to go.

Mostly, we talked about classmates. He told me about one friend, later a roommate at Harvard, whom I remembered mostly for his grinning indifference to just about everything: he would be an antiwar leader as a medical student at Columbia, Lloyd told me—while Lloyd was a law student there—then a professor of emergency medicine at BU ("a pioneer in his field, from what I understand"). And about another, Lloyd's closest friend at St. Paul's, also a Harvard roommate and godfather to his son, who had died of retinal cancer eleven years earlier with Lloyd in the room at his side. ("His wife asked me to give a eulogy," Lloyd would write me later in an email. "I ended with a memory from school—the Sunday evensong prayer: 'Oh Lord, support us all the day long until the shadows lengthen and the evening comes . . .' Steve wasn't particularly religious, but he liked Sunday evensong, as I did also. That prayer echoes with me still.")

I shared with him what I'd learned of Chad Floyd, whom I'd seen the week before—that he'd enlisted in the Marine Corps three months out of Yale, had been a platoon leader in Vietnam and was now married with two kids, was an architect and part-time jazz drummer. We spoke of Philip Heckscher, who'd also gone on to Harvard with Lloyd, then had spent twenty years teaching grade-schoolers in New York. And John Cocroft, whom I would be meeting for the first time the next morning in Providence.

But for all that, not a lot was said. I was careful. We both were careful, though it's hard to say just why. I suppose, for me, because we'd had our roles once—at the top and bottom of things, more or less—and as long ago as that had been, and as meaningless as it should have been now, forty-four years later in the Harvard Club bar, it was still the only real basis we had. He was the president, taller and stronger and a hundred times surer; and I was the skinny, anxious kid who talked too much, tried too hard, and dropped batons. Ghosts that old and deeply dug can take longer than a night to die.

Neither of us mentioned Arthur, who was still alive at the time and emailing furiously. Or Rich, who had died in a hospice twelve days before—though we wouldn't know this for months. The only reference to John Kerry came when Lloyd asked if I'd read the magazine article, written a month or two before, about John being booed at the fortieth class reunion. I said yes, that I'd read it. Lloyd said it hadn't happened, that he'd been there himself—had made the toast himself, as president—and that John had not been booed.

He told me this twice: at the beginning of the evening, then again at the end. It had happened on his watch. He was still our president. It was important that I understood.

TWELVE HOURS LATER, I WOULD BE sitting with John Cocroft in the Café Roma in Providence and he would be telling me about his fears of failing, his hatred of expectations, and the night he left his necktie behind. And I would drive home three hours later wondering how it could happen that two boys, two people, could come from so much the same place, be so very alike in so many obvious manifestations—smart, decent, athletic, likable, well liked—and yet one be unsure and fearful, the other so naturally golden, so free of heavy weights. I would wonder this all the way home, and still never get past where I started: that some things just aren't knowable, and that probably, in any case, there were things I didn't yet know.

I was right about the second part, at least in the case of Lloyd.

IT WAS TWO MONTHS BEFORE WE got together again. This time it would be for dinner: at a small, colonial-era inn fifteen miles west of Boston, not far, Lloyd had told me, from where his married daughter lived. We had arranged to meet first in the bar, which was dark and low-ceilinged and smelled of beer and old wood, where we talked for half an hour about the recent troubles of St.

Paul's: a boy had drowned in the pool on campus, the rector of ten years had recently been let go by the board.

Lloyd seemed much as before: warm and gracious and happy enough to be there, but also very measured—almost judge-like—with his words. I began to feel daunted by this: impatient, pulled between roles, unsure of how to move our time along. Like being stuck in a second language you've known forever but haven't used in a while.

We moved from the bar to the dining room, where we ordered our meal right away. It couldn't be a late night, Lloyd had told me; he had an early-morning appointment in Boston, and a long day on top of that. Almost before the waiter had left the table with our orders, he looked at me, smiled thinly, almost politely, and announced:

"Third-form year was tough for me. It was awful, actually."

I didn't know how to react. I said that I hadn't known, that I never would have guessed. He said he thought probably no one had known at the time: "I couldn't have done that. It was too painful and awkward to ever talk about."

This opened a dialogue, which led gradually into a monologue, which stretched over the rest of our evening. Then another evening that followed—nine months later, also at our Concord inn—and several long emails in between. I don't know what made him tell me what he did. It hadn't been prompted; there was no way he could have thought I knew. And he isn't (unlike John Cocroft) a person you'd ever think of as impulsive or unguarded. Maybe, in his lawyerly way, he had gone through the process of concluding that my efforts at biography deserved a full disclosure. Or perhaps he drew some satisfaction in the unburdening. However it happened, it seemed clear to me that he had made up his mind before arriving for dinner that I should know the truth of his troubles at St. Paul's.

It began with the story of third-form year, his first year at the school. The longer he talked, the softer, the less judge-like—the more like a classmate—he came to seem to me. And the harder it got to suppress my amazement (I had last seen John, at that point, only a week or so before) at the echo it seemed I was hearing.

"I was scared. From the first day, just really scared. There were all these smart people, so many brilliant people—and then I failed math and Latin my first fortnight, failed them both. I couldn't figure out some of the assignments, and I couldn't ask anyone for help. I was just lost—I thought there was a real chance I was going to flunk out of school. Max's [his roommate's] name for me was 'Big Dumb Lloydy'—and I *felt* dumb, I felt inadequate, like I was in way over my head . . .

"Then my hair started falling out from this infection I got from my football helmet—this 'accidental baldness,' now my hair is falling out in clumps. It was awful, undignified. There was no dignity at all, none. And I was homesick. Badly, acutely homesick. I don't think I've ever felt so vulnerable in my life."

Then he told me about his uncle. And about the plaque—dark gray stone, with a hand-carved message—that I'd walked by five hundred times but had never noticed much less read, on the wall of the hallway leading to the chapel at St. Paul's:

With Enduring Love
Lieutenant (jg) Demarest Lloyd II
July 11, 1919–June 12, 1944
USNA Fighter Squadron 2, Attached to USS Hornet
Killed in Action over Guam
President, Sixth Form 1938
"Ye Shall Know the Truth, and the Truth Shall Set You Free"

He had been Lloyd's mother's brother. A champion sailor, hockey player, sixth-form president, Harvard class of '42—dead at twenty-five, thirty-two days after Lloyd had come into the world. For years before Lloyd had arrived at St. Paul's, his plaque had hung in that hallway—where it hangs today—passed twice every morning by every boy in the school. He had been a presence in Lloyd's life just as long.

"He was everywhere. The sense of him was everywhere, I knew all these things about him—I knew I'd had this incredible uncle, and that he'd died for this important cause. Growing up, that was a pretty big part of my world."

He was christened Lloyd MacDonald. When he was ten years old, living in New Bedford, Massachusetts, with his parents now divorced, his mother changed his name. He was now *Demarest* Lloyd MacDonald, after his dead uncle. She wrote a letter to his fifth-grade teacher asking that he henceforth be called by that name.

"And they did. They started calling me that. I was mortified. It wasn't me—I was 'Lloyd.' But I didn't think I could complain."

The "Demarest" didn't stick (he is today officially D. Lloyd MacDonald, and has always since gone by "Lloyd"), but the weight of the legacy did. In his seventh-grade American history class, he remembers (and his recording of these memories is so vivid sometimes, and so precisely rendered, that he could be talking about last week), his choice of "The History of the Second World War" as a term-paper topic was not made casually:

"My uncle had been a hero, a true, tragic family hero. Everything about that war, the war he had died in, became a kind of inspiration to me."

SOMEWHERE ALONG THE LINE, however such things happen in the mind of a teenage boy, the war seems to have become for Lloyd a metaphor for struggle. Any sort of honest struggle, as long as it had to do with sacrifice or steadfastness or personal prevailing. Churchill was an early hero. Teddy Roosevelt was another. *The Red Badge of Courage* was his favorite book as a teen.

This is a theme that will come up several times during our dinners. The words he will use for it will vary only slightly—always some close version of what he will call it that night: "the redemptive power of hardship as proof of dignity."

Listening to him through all of this—dignity, redemption, the iconic fighter-pilot uncle—it begins after a while to sound oddly outdated to me. Like talk of the Depression, or Horatio Alger or Audie Murphy, or being "red-blooded," or walking five miles to school through the snow every day. Very old-worldly, very righteous, very male. World War Two has stopped being our template for warfare; I don't know how many people read *The Red Badge of Courage* anymore.

But these were breathing values in 1958. My father still rhapsodized at the dinner table about the "lessons of the Depression"; the war was recent history, Churchill was a demigod to anyone you asked. And probably no one would have questioned the wisdom of renaming a ten-year-old after an uncle who had died, a week after D-Day, flying spitfires against the Japanese.

St. Paul's was a bastion of all this. Stoicism, fortitude, temperance. The manly virtues. And for a boy arriving with a dead war hero sitting on his shoulder, and doubts about how brave or bright or capable he might be, it's not hard to see how the school could have been the perfect crucible: a forging ground for the blessings of struggle, an affirmation—if successful—against a lifetime of self-doubt.

"It exposed me," Lloyd will say to me toward the end

of our last evening together. "I didn't know who I was, or what mattered to me. It exposed me to myself."

But in the meantime, as he has told me already by then, his time at St. Paul's was a succession of terrors.

"Coming back from Christmas vacation in 1959—I'll never forget it, it had to be one of the worst days of my life. My mother drove me to the train in the dark, she dropped me off in the dark and said good-bye. I didn't think it was possible to feel that scared or alone . . .

"It was awful, terrible. Here I am, the namesake of this war hero and SPS class president, this person I've been revering my whole life. And I'm scared and I'm lonely, I'm worried about flunking out—I figure there isn't anyone in the class who isn't smarter than me."

And two years later he's voted sixth-form president (taking after his uncle); he wins the school football medal, goes on to Harvard, becomes a lawyer, runs for DA, is named by the governor to sit as a federal judge.

There's no telling how this sort of thing happens: what exactly is the difference between a frightened, self-doubting kid who gets elected class president, then goes on to conquer the world, and another in the same class, also frightened but able, who just abdicates, then spends a lifetime looking back. There's no knowing which one will be which, or what big or little thing will make the difference.

In Lloyd's case, though, it's pretty plain that his uncle was an enormous presence—it's hard to imagine another that could have been the equal of that. But it was the school itself, he will tell me, that was the difference in the end.

He found a mentor fourth-form year, a history teacher named Tom Buell. ("He was the turning point—he was the one who got me excited, really, viscerally excited, about government and politics. And he listened. He related to what I wanted to do with my life. He asked my opinion about things. He helped me believe in myself.") His grades improved. He made his club football team that year. He won the top prize in the school for his knowledge of current events.

And all the while this was happening, he was reading Churchill's letters and Teddy Roosevelt's essays (a collection called *The Strenuous Life*. "Its theme was similar, and very powerful, the redemptive power of hardship, our effort to overcome it . . .") and listening to our rector, Matthew Warren, every morning in chapel calling on his boys to rise above themselves. And for Lloyd, it was a powerful mix.

"I remember very explicitly, Matt Warren telling us from his pulpit, '*You are St. Paul's boys.*' And there was never any doubt in my mind what he meant by that. He was telling us it was a high calling, a serious calling, that we were expected to make a *difference in the world* . . .

"Those were high expectations. *Enormous* expectations. It seemed like an important message to me, a kind of noble message. And I just took it really seriously. Even at fourteen."

That may have been where it all began for Lloyd—"You are St. Paul's boys"—and probably for others as well. It was a refrain we all heard constantly, both explicitly and by suggestion: We were different, we were special; we'd been smiled upon by birth and providence, and therefore owed an extra measure back. It was everywhere, like background music, or the smell of the air or the food. We woke and slept with it.

Some boys, like Lloyd—a minority, but not as small as you'd think—took it and fashioned the beginnings of a belief system, and from that the beginnings of a life. Others, like the Regs (at least for those three or four years of their Reg-dom), heard a different message, my father's message—in some cases, *their* fathers' message—an off-key version of that same refrain: We were *better* than others, superior by birth and breeding, and entitled therefore to look down. These weren't the majority, either; but they set a standard and created a language that drove day-to-day life for far too many of us.

And there were those, too, for whom the message, for whatever reasons, seemed less a challenge than a rebuke: the expectations were *too* great, the bar too high to ever clear. And for such as these, if life continued to deliver that message, the world could come to seem very cruel.

THEN THERE WAS ARTHUR—as far from being a "St. Paul's boy" as any boy, before or since, who ever attended the school. The news of his death was six months old by the time Lloyd and I would meet for our last dinner in Concord. Of the dozens of classmates' emails that had followed it, none had seemed more thoughtful, or more honestly stricken, than Lloyd's.

He had opened with a rambling recollection of how he'd first heard of Arthur, from a family friend who'd been at the school with him—as I had—the year before Lloyd had arrived. ("He told me about this giant kid from the sticks who was bigger and stronger than anyone in the next two forms . . . who had actually had sex—'gone all the way'—with a girl.") He went on to reprise the degradations, including the toilet memory ("[Arthur] in that iced-over expanse while the rest of us passed by and laughed and gawked . . ."), and another nearly as execrable, which he described in detail and admitted his part in: "It has ever after bothered me." He wrote also of the letter, years before—sometime in the 1970s, he thinks—in which Arthur had written him that St. Paul's was an "unChristian place." He wrote about meanness, and forgiveness, and said he was ashamed. He closed by saying he thought that Arthur—"who touched me deeply, in part by instilling a sense of shame"—was the most memorable boy in the class.

I ask him about all this now, toward the end of our last dinner together. "It could be a cruel place, a hard place," he says. "It depended on who you were. For Arthur it was cruel." Then he tells me again what he had written already in his email: that when he'd read *Lord of the Flies* several years later, in college, he had thought first of St. Paul's, and of Arthur, and recognized himself.

"The school *broke* some people, it made others," he will say to me later as we are walking back to our cars following dinner that night. "It *made* me."

LLOYD WAS AT COLUMBIA LAW SCHOOL, a month short of graduation, when he got his induction notice in the spring of 1969. He was ordered to report to the Boston Navy Yard that July. There were 540,000 troops in Vietnam by that time; his brother was one of them. More than 33,000 were dead already. John Kerry, wounded three times, the last time on the Bai Hap River in March, by now was on reassignment in Brooklyn. Peter Johnson had been dead for a year.

Vietnam isn't one of Lloyd's favorite subjects. He reported to Boston that July, but ended up not serving—deferred, he says, because of a blown-out knee from playing rugby at Harvard, and because of an asthma condition. He is direct when I ask him about it, toward the end of our first dinner, but very clipped in his response. His discomfort with the subject seems plain.

"I was against the war, but I would have gone. Peter was dead, my brother was there, my uncle had died as a soldier, a friend from Harvard had lost both of his legs—and I was being excused for a rugby injury. Let's just say it's not something I'm very proud of."

His edginess surprises me, but it probably shouldn't.

He's a very old-world sort of person, almost a throwback in some ways. Duty, honor, justice, patriotism, continuity: these are the things that seem to shape him—that hasn't changed since St. Paul's. He is a moralist in this way. He seems born to be a judge.

The law may be his favorite subject. He changes when he talks about it. He sits up straighter, talks faster, smiles wider and more readily. He tells me, proudly and almost without prompting, about his earliest days in the Suffolk County DA's office in Boston in the early seventies and how, as the new kid in the office, he got handed all the weakest cases that came in ("Shit rolls downhill" was how his boss put it to him at the time) and lost the first seven that he tried, then never lost another after that.

"They called me the turnaround kid," he says. He is smiling and shaking his head in remembrance. It is a side of Lloyd I haven't yet seen.

"I love the courtroom," he has said to me just before this (seeming almost to have forgotten about his judgeship, his recent change in roles). "I love everything about it. I love working with witnesses, I love working with cops. It's stimulating, it's competitive, there are winners and losers, you find out pretty quick where you stand."

But you don't have to listen long to find out that there's more to it than that. And when he starts talking about the rightness of the law—the "sense of mission" he felt in those days—it begins to sound very close to what I've been hearing about the rector's old sermons at school:

"I was doing important work. Crime was a big problem [in Boston] in the seventies. Putting bad guys in jail was something that mattered, that made life better. It was enormously satisfying for me."

All that ended in 1982, when he ran for Suffolk County DA. He lost—"got buried"—in the Democratic primary, and would never run for elective office again. There was something about that defeat, maybe the nearly two-to-one margin, maybe his naivete about his chances to begin with, or just the public nature of it all—he never really says—that was personal for him, and remains so, at least in memory, nearly twenty-five years later.

"I felt exposed. I felt incompetent, utterly incompetent. It was something I wouldn't wish on anyone. The anxiety of it some days—hard to describe, just really, really bad. A lot like third-form year at SPS, I felt the same way sometimes—the same kinds of fears and worries, of just being so totally outdone, so totally exposed as a failure. I thought of that a lot at the time. The lesson was really helpful."

He went into private practice after that, and by 1990 was a partner in the Boston office of a large national firm. His specialty, unlike the early years, was civil litigation, often involving aspects of white-collar crime: fraud, insider trading, violations of environmental law. He stayed until late 2004, not long after we were first in touch, when he was named an associate justice of the state superior court.

In the meantime his marriage had ended. Even by

our second long dinner together, there isn't much he'll say about this. They were married twenty-three years and had a son and a daughter. She was French, and returned to France when it was over.

"She left me" is how he sums it up. "It was her doing, her decision. It was a very hard time in my life."

He is close to both his children. His daughter, whom he describes as a "whiz kid"—and whose house he has just come from when we meet for dinner those nights—is married with two children and lives just west of Boston. His son, Jeremy, now just past thirty, is another story. When he talks about him, there is a softness, a tenderness almost, that hasn't come across at any other time in our talks:

"He's had his troubles. He was dyslexic, he couldn't read at six. There were several colleges. I had a lot of trouble dealing with it, with him. He was a real wise-ass for a while."

The longer he goes on, the clearer it becomes to me that Jeremy's troubles have hit very close to the core:

"He suffered, he really did. It took a long time for me to see that—I just didn't get it for a while. In the end he was okay, he got it together. He had this incredible . . . epiphany, I guess you'd have to call it, when he was in his early twenties. He just sort of saw the light. And he's landed on his feet. He graduated two years ago from MIT . . .

"But I learned from that. It was a struggle for a while. It's always a struggle when it's your own kid, I guess—and he was *tough*. But I managed it. I came to feel the hurt . . ."

WE WILL TALK ANOTHER FEW MINUTES after this: about his son, his daughter, his grandkids, and one or two classmates we haven't covered before—then pay the check and walk outside to our cars. It is a warm June night; he doesn't seem in a hurry. Neither am I. Somewhere along the line he has stopped being The President. At least for now, he is only my classmate. And a warm and decent man. And still the perfect judge.

The next morning I get an email, with the subject line of "Good time last night." He writes that he enjoyed our talk—that it got him thinking some more on the ride home to Boston: about the school and himself, "and my place in the world, and where some of those values come from."

He closes by quoting several lines from a prayer in the St. Paul's prayer book ("Keep alive in our hearts, we beseech thee, that adventurous spirit which makes men scorn the way of safety."), which he says is one of his favorites. It isn't one I recall. He says he keeps the prayer book close at hand, that it is a source of some comfort for him.

"Anyway, you got me thinking, not just reminiscing. It was fun."

My Father, Myself

It is my fourth graduation day. The other three before this have all been gorgeous and sunny; the rector last year began by thanking the Lord for being so cooperative. He couldn't have said that today. There are heavy clouds, and it is almost cold.

My cousin Stuart is graduating today. My aunt and uncle are here to watch it happen; we'll probably all go out to supper together before they take him home. Two years ago it was Stuart's brother—we went out to supper that year. Ten years ago my brother Jimmy graduated; and Archie four years before that. And their fathers, of course—my uncle and father—and there will be more to come. Next year is supposed to be mine.

But it won't be. I won't be here next year. Today, or maybe tomorrow, will be my last day at the school. I think I might know this already (there is plenty of reason to think it); I think it may be the reason I'll always remember the weather, and what sixth-formers I say good-bye to outside of the chapel, and what the speaker says. But no one has told me so yet.

The chapel lawn is a sea of chairs. I am halfway back from the stage, toward the outside of a row of other fifth-formers, with a good view of things. The speaker is some sort of public person, a politician maybe. He is younger than usual for a graduation speaker; his hair is still dark, he stands very straight and speaks in a clear, strong voice that carries to the back of the lawn. He is talking about Lazarus, the poor man from the parable by Luke. He reads the parable through, or at least the first part of it—about the rich man being clothed in fine linen and eating like a king, and the poor man at his gate with his sores being licked by dogs—then says something about the burden of being rich and privileged and the expectations that come with being graduates of St. Paul's.

But then he changes course—or maybe it was his course all along, I'm not sure—and asks a question rhetorically: Do we notice anything in particular about what we're told about these two men? Four or five seconds pass. Then he answers the question: Lazarus has a name—"He will always be Lazarus." The rich man is only the rich man, forever nameless, remembered by no one at all.

I am dazzled by this, and will ponder it for weeks. I'm not sure I even know why.

A week or two later, my father will get this letter from the rector:

"I feel that the school will have to drop Geoff. He has not been helpful throughout the year, has constantly resented the pressure we have had to apply to get his work done; we have had a long history with him of this kind of thing, and have regretfully come to the conclusion that he should not be permitted to return." It will go on to speak of my "surliness and resentment and uncooperative attitude," then to express the rector's deep regrets.

This will be crushing news for my father. He is a graduate of the class of 1922; his younger brother, then his first and second sons, have followed in order—then have gone on, in family fashion, to Yale. He will tell me, his third son, on receiving the letter, that I have placed a "stigma" on the family name that can never be fully erased.

For a time, I will believe him. Then I won't. My St. Paul's years, as time goes by, will grow dimmer and less heavy in remembering. A generation will pass, then most of another. By the time John Kerry runs for president—and the emails start up, then Rich and Arthur die—I will have almost forgotten our class president's first name.

IN A FRAMED BLACK-AND-WHITE PHOTO that hangs over my desk, a tall, thin, dark-haired young man in a striped shirt and khaki pants stands next to a shorter, much older man in suspenders and a wide-brimmed brown felt hat. There are tall corn stalks in the background. The younger man looks very intense and purposeful; he is turned toward the older one, who is looking up at him.

The photo was taken by the Associated Press of West Virginia in July of 1969. The younger man is me. I'd arrived that afternoon at the home of Clyde and Polly Robinette and their eight or nine children, alongside a creek in Mingo County, West Virginia, a mile east of the Kentucky border, where I would live the next five weeks.

I was paying eighteen dollars a day for the privilege, about what you'd pay for a decent hotel room at the time—which was the only reason the Associated Press was there. And the *New York Times* and the *Wall Street Journal* and a dozen or so more. I was "the 25 year-old college student from a comfortable home for four," paying Hilton rates to live in poverty. (It hadn't been my idea; a local antipoverty office had advertised the offer—"an opportunity to experience firsthand the problems of the Appalachian poor"—and I was one of the few to sign on. The media, which was wild for the story, had no one else to interview or film.) A day or two later, I would be featured two nights running on *The Huntley-Brinkley Report*—talking soberly about illiteracy and coal-mine safety while I tried, comically, to milk a cow.

The reporters left the second day I was there. That same night, we sat down to our first supper together: thirteen or fourteen of us, including a grandfather and an unmarried daughter's infant child, around the big table in the Robinettes' kitchen. No one spoke through most of that supper—the loudest sounds were the clinking of dishes and the background slurps of a badly retarded daughter. And I saw, for the first time since my arrival, the fool I'd let myself be. It's part of the reason for that photo over my desk.

I learned many things in those five weeks: about ignorance and inbreeding, tent-meeting evangelism, black-lung disease, the power and politics of the mines. Also about trust and kindness, and dead-end despair: how a life can be over, still with two-thirds left to live, at twenty-three or twenty-four.

The Robinettes had a daughter, Shirley, who was about that age. Shirley was smart and blond and very pretty, and with a brimming-over hunger for life. But she had that little baby, and no husband and no money, and the saddest eyes you've ever seen. We used to sit outside on the porch after supper, sometimes until long after dark, sometimes with Polly and other times not, and Shirley would rock her baby in her lap and ask me questions: about New York, Boston, California, elevators, taxis, rock concerts, airplanes, art museums, and a thousand other things. And I would do my best to answer, then tell her—nearly always, at some point before the evening was done—that she ought to come to New York and visit, that I'd find her a place to stay and show her the city myself. And always she would say that she would.

(I don't know, in the end, what became of Shirley. I did get a call from her a year or so later; she said she'd won a contest of some sort, sponsored by a detergent company, I think, and that the prize was a trip to New York, where I was still living at the time. She said she was calling from outside of the city—somewhere on Long Island, near the airport—that she'd been there for the weekend already and would be flying home the next day. I asked her to meet me for dinner. She said that she couldn't, that she just wanted me to know she'd kept her promise to come. She sounded very shy and nervous on the phone, and was clearly in a hurry to hang up. I never heard from her again.)

I was angry by the time I left Appalachia: at the mining companies, the media, the universe, myself. I went home to New York, where I was living alone on West Tenth Street in the Village (I never learned the origins of that "comfortable home for four"), and wrote my anger down, along with some of the things I had learned. A short, unpaid-for essay—my first bylined piece—appeared at the end of that summer in an Appalachian journal called *Mountain Life and Work*. A much longer one, nearly four thousand words, maybe the longest piece of writing I'd ever completed at that time—and rewritten, torturously, half a dozen times—was published in the Sunday magazine section of the *Louisville Courier-Journal* eight months later, in April of 1970. The check I got, for $150, went uncashed until early summer, pressed between the pages of a biography of Jack London. I would take it out from time to time, just to look at it, to examine the signature and the writing of my name.

I graduated from college that same summer—State University of New York at Stony Brook, the last of three—bought a used Ford Econoline van and, with my girlfriend, spent eight weeks driving between state parks and Apache reservations and eight-dollar motels from New Jersey to Oregon and back. I'd just gotten my first credit card—Carte Blanche—and my first dog, Phoebe, an ugly blond little mutt I would somehow manage to love and keep safe through seven homes and sixteen years. And I was a writer now. Life for once seemed almost uncomplicated.

I HAD BEEN GONE BY THEN nine years from St. Paul's, nearly all of them spent bumping around between colleges, or else between college and life. (I was briefly, at one time or another, an insurance salesman, a speed-reading teacher, cabdriver, waiter, and employment agent, none for more than five months.) My father had died at the start of those years—when I was eighteen, of liver failure brought on by the alcoholism that was also responsible, only a little less directly, for a lot of other things. He was a bully and a bigot, a failed stockbroker, and the worst sort of husband to my mother, who had ended her life with an overdose of sleeping pills when I was nine years old. He had remarried soon after, to his former lover, and stayed married to her till he died. I'd been away at school through nearly all of that time: first at Fay School in Massachusetts, where I was sent when I was ten, then for four years—intended to be five—at St. Paul's.

Last came a year at a little school in Massachusetts, called Lenox, the only school that would accept me after my expulsion, and a plainer place by far. It was at Lenox that I first learned to wash dishes and rake leaves till my shoulders ached, and sit up late talking about things I really did feel or fear. I had friends at Lenox; I played on the tennis team, I acted in plays, I invited a Spanish girl to a tea dance and kissed her in full view. My favorite teacher was a former drill instructor named Nol Putnam who had a flat-top haircut and would scream at you red-faced, publicly, when you were rude or selfish, then invite you to his home an hour later for pizza and a Coke.

June came. I'd been accepted at several colleges, even some good ones. But not at Yale—"the only college for a son of mine," according to my father, whom I feared far too much to defy. And so it was settled. I enlisted in the air force two weeks later, arrived by bus at Lackland Air Force Base in San Antonio on my eighteenth birthday, July 1, 1962.

I was there two months. It was hot and filthy; I was one of only three or four whites in our flight of about eighty, all of us from New York—I'd almost never before known a black person who didn't work in someone's yard or kitchen. The drill instructor, named Hudson, who was white and from Maine, called me "Little Richie" loudly and publicly fifteen or twenty times a day, and made me scream out the lines, "My name is Little Richie and I'm from *Tuxedo Pa-wwwk,* New York!" (My father and new stepmother were living by then in Tuxedo Park, a gated community an hour northwest of the city.) When I failed to scream them loud enough, he'd make me do pushups with his boot on the back of my neck until I was ready to throw up.

Basic training ended the last week of August. At the "graduation" ceremony the final day, with all of us lined up at attention to get our first stripes, Hudson, with an officer beside him, put his mouth to my ear and whispered very softly, *"You got good guts."* That same day or the next one, we got our orders; I was to report to Biloxi, Mississippi, for firefighters' school. I assumed there'd been a mistake: The recruiter in New York had assured me that, if I passed the necessary tests, I'd be sent to the air force language school in California. And I had passed the tests.

I refused to go to Biloxi; the air force refused to give in. I was released—as "psychologically unadaptable"—the first week of September, given my pay, and sent home.

It was the first time in my life I'd been paid for anything. I was proud of the money, proud of Hudson's whispered words to me, and proudest of all of the principled stand I had taken. I arrived home, still with my cash and my pride, a day or so later. My father gave me $100 and told me to pack and be gone by the morning. I was a quitter, he said. He wasn't going to have a quitter for a son.

I've sometimes thought of that week, in a very real way, as the beginning of my life. I left the next day on a bus from Port Authority in New York to Denver, then made my way west to Aspen, where I had the notion that I'd spend the winter as a ski bum. I was a decent enough skier; but except for that summer in Texas, I'd never in my life been west of New Jersey, had never held a job, and had very little idea, outside of the skiing part, just what a ski bum was or did. I got hired, though, almost right away (it was still September, the off-season, and Aspen was still a small town), at a local lumber company, then was fired three days later when I backed their truck into a freight car I was supposed to help unload. (I'd never really learned to drive.) So I made my way back to Denver, where I got hired by the Collier's company to sell encyclopedias door to door. I went on sales calls every night for two weeks—my territory was Colorado Springs—and never sold a page. I skipped out on my bill at the Y, sold the old Buick I'd just bought for $50, and got a bus to Longmont, thirty miles north, where someone had told me there was work.

It was October by this time. I spent the next two weeks with a work crew in Longmont, laying a new roof on the local high school until the hot tar took the skin off my face. Then I sat for two days on an old sofa in front of the TV in the manager's office of the boarding-house where I was staying, with salve all over my face, watching Khrushchev's ships close the distance on JFK's Cuba blockade. People were talking about war and basement bomb shelters and overnight call-ups of troops. Everybody was scared. *I* was scared, but also felt very alive. On the day before the crisis ended, I made a call to a local recruiter (I was too embarrassed to go in person) to ask whether "psychologically unadaptable" could be considered in time of war. But he was too busy to talk to me.

It felt to me, almost every day that fall, that I was waking up to a different person in my skin. I'd never felt so alive, or so certain of myself—what we'd probably today call "empowered." I never went back to work on the high-school roof. A week after the Cuban crisis ended, I was in Kimball, Nebraska, pulling twelve-hour shifts in an oil-field work-over unit for $11 an hour (three or four times what I'd been making up to then), measuring my manhood in barfights on weekends, and quoting Kerouac to five-dollar whores. When that was over—it was late November by then—I hitchhiked to California, where I stayed for ten days as a lay brother in a monastery in Big Sur, building cells and folding laundry for three dollars a day. When I wasn't working, I read: Kerouac, Jack London, D. H.

Lawrence, Hemingway, Agee, Maugham, Saroyan, Kahlil Gibran. I kept my books, along with almost $500 I'd saved from the oil fields, in a straw shoulder bag the monastery brothers had taught me how to weave. I stayed up late and woke early. I was very proud of myself.

At night sometimes, I would watch the meteor showers over the coastline, and talk with the other brothers about the meaning of God and life. One night as we were watching, one of them told me he thought I should go home, in time for Christmas, and try to make peace with my father and his wife. "Christmas is a time for forgiveness. And you only have one father," he said—which for some reason seemed very wise to me at the time.

I ARRIVED BACK IN MID-DECEMBER. THE brother in Big Sur had missed his guess—my father wanted nothing to do with me, ordered me out of the house almost as soon as I'd arrived. So I went into New York, got a room at the Y on West Thirty-fourth Street and a two-week job selling ski equipment to holiday shoppers in an off–Fifth Avenue store.

I tried again on Christmas Eve: took a bus out of the city, then walked from the bus stop to the house where my father was living with his wife. It was the last time I would see him alone. I would tell the story, nearly forty years later, in my first published book, a memoir of my childhood and my parents' fractured lives:

He was living now in Tuxedo Park, an iron-gated enclave of dwindling old money an hour outside of New York. The house was enormous, Tudor-style, with a circular driveway, a landscaped garden in back and a third floor of maids' rooms. Bea [our cook] was still with him, as was Russell the butler, Steve the gardener and chambermaids who came and went. Mrs. Coe was still Mrs. Douglas. They had been married nearly eight years . . .

He was at home alone when I arrived. In his library, drunk and crying and talking to himself. It was his mawkish mode . . . He threw his arms around my neck, pulled me to the couch and covered my face with scratchy kisses. He'd been a "wretched father," he said. He begged me to forgive him. I told him there was nothing to forgive. At the time, I believed it.

He said then that he had no friends. This seemed extreme to me and I told him so. I named several people I considered his friends. "Not real friends," he said. He was sobbing so hard I could barely make out his words.

I argued with him. I pitied him—the first time I had ever really pitied him—and tried to offer comfort. But my message was empty, and he knew it. His power was gone for me. I wanted only to be gone. Then he said something I had never thought before—and never would have. But I knew it was right the instant I heard it:

"Everybody loves me, nobody respects me. For God's sake, Geoffrey, don't turn out like me."

I couldn't answer, and didn't. I think he heard my silence. Absurdly, he made me swear not to be like him. I'd have sworn to anything just to be out of the room.

I saw him again the next morning—Christmas day—and once more that night at Granny's party. Again, he was drunk—more likely, still drunk—but ascendant now, at the top of his powers. Before dinner and after, he gave toasts and told jokes to all comers. "Wensceslaus" [an anti-Jew joke, a Christmas favorite] had never drawn a bigger crowd. He barely looked my way all night.

Two days later he went into the hospital with stomach pains. I never saw him again.

I wanted to go west again after the funeral. I had no idea where, or for what, but I'd felt a sense of myself, of things in general, when I was in Colorado and Nebraska, that I now missed badly, had missed from the moment I got back. And my father's death had flattened me, had left me dumb and confused and angry, with nothing to do with any of it but try not to let it show. I felt misplaced.

But the family stepped in. An uncle in Connecticut, my father's brother, a decent, forbearing man with three sons around my age and a wife with the world's warmest heart, had been named—by family consensus—my new guardian. We had a talk, the morning after the funeral in the library of his home. He listened to everything I said, all the way through, nodding his head often, then pointed out to me—gently, almost tenderly, in a way that would have been unthinkable from my father—that while a "wanderlust" was understandable in a young man of eighteen, it was time now to think about college and life. I was so grateful for his patience, and for what felt like understanding, that I gave way without a fight.

(I should say something about money. I had some: roughly $250,000, in trust from my parents, with about the same amount still to come from my grandmother—my father's mother—who would die a year later at the age of ninety-three. Part of my uncle's role with me, from the time of my father's death until his own fifteen years later, was as an executor of these trusts. He was a conservative man by nature, and sparing in what he allotted. But I had what was needed. There was never a question of means.)

I was enrolled two weeks later, in February 1963, at Centre College in Danville, Kentucky. It was a small, well-regarded, very Southern sort of place—chosen both for its willingness to take me on a week's notice and for its proximity to my half-brother Archie, fourteen years older than I was and already married with three kids, who lived in Louisville, about ninety minutes northwest, and who—or so the thinking went—could keep an eye on me. (Archie, my father's oldest son by his first marriage, had been in the class of 1948 at St. Paul's: an almost-legendary athlete, one of the best ever at the school, still recalled reverently fourteen years after he had left. I barely knew him growing up, though I knew all the stories by heart. He'd been a hero from the time I was old enough to tie my shoes.)

I went to the racetrack most afternoons that first semester, and played poker almost every night; by the end of a month, I owed money to every kid in the game. That summer I took a factory job in Louisville, to help reimburse my uncle for paying off my gambling debts (he didn't think it right to pay them from the trust), then got fired after a month for playing poker in the warehouse on company time. I went back to Centre in September, fell in love with a dark-haired girl named Gabriella—from Massachusetts, one of the only other northerners there—in the dining hall the second day of school, and almost never went to another class. Midterm grades were posted the third week of November; I had an F in every course.

The president was assassinated that same afternoon. Gabriella told me that night after supper that she didn't want to see me anymore. I took her back to her dorm at eleven, went to the apartment of the dean of men, and told him I was dropping out. Archie picked me up the next morning. All he remembers me talking about, in the car on the way back to Louisville, were the hickies on my neck.

It was a terrible time. I went back the same week to

my uncle's in Connecticut—it was late November now—where I got drunk every night on warm bourbon, made lovesick phone calls to Gabriella in Kentucky, then either drove to Danbury and got myself in barfights or made calls to the homes of oil workers I remembered from my time in Nebraska, who had usually forgotten my name.

Three days into the new year—1964—under pressure from my uncle and a psychiatrist I'd been seeing in New York, I signed myself in to the Institute of Living in Hartford, Connecticut. I was there exactly six months. My doctor, short and skinny and not much older than thirty, asked me endless questions about my mother (fewer about my father, who had died only twelve months before), also about my dreams, my gambling and drinking, and what he called my need to "play chicken with life."

I don't think much was solved in those sessions, or by the Institute itself. It sobered me—to wake up in a mental hospital every day—and forced me to think about things, like my father's power over me and why my mother might have chosen to die, that I'd never considered before. And I met some memorable, very damaged people: a beautiful nineteen-year-old prodigy named Pam—she called herself Gopher—who looked like the early Greta Garbo, could read a full-length novel in an hour, and spoke effortlessly, for our amusement, in spontaneous rhymed couplets, but couldn't be trusted with a fork or a pencil and had hard black scars on her wrists and forearms—and later her eyelids—from the stubbing out of cigarettes; and Wyman, a classmate of Archie's at

St. Paul's, who'd been an animal collector on five continents, never stopped joking, and was unbeatable at Ping-Pong and nine-ball, but wore the same unwashed clothes until they rotted apart, and shot himself to death in a rented apartment a month after being discharged. (He had written a memoir—a hundred pages, about sheiks and princes and polar bears, the whole business of traveling the world in quest of animals for zoos—that he'd given me and asked me to rewrite. I'd promised him I would. I still have it, in a yellow folder at the bottom of a suitcase. I haven't looked at it in years, but I don't think I could ever throw it out.)

I left the Institute in June. In September I was back at Centre. Things were different now. I'd made promises: to my uncle, my brother Archie, and the dean of men, who'd vouched for me with the Admissions people to get me a second chance and asked me, plainly and kindly, my first night back on campus, to please not prove him wrong. I tried hard not to. I stayed away from Gabriella and away from poker games, and went only on weekends to the track. I roomed with a football player, a big lug named Lowell who drank way too much—it would kill him at thirty-two—and had his troubles in the classroom, but took care of me like a brother that year. (If I close my eyes and conjure Lowell at St. Paul's, he is Arthur with an upgrade in hygiene.) I played on the tennis team, went to luaus at the Beta House, gave my family-crest ring to a brown-haired junior from eastern Kentucky who gave me things I'd never been given before.

I should have stayed, but I didn't. I was reading too much, for one thing: Camus and Sartre, Lawrence, Golding, Vonnegut, Ayn Rand—*city* writers, writing about sex and angst, suicide, rebellion, all sorts of city things. And Dylan was at the Bitter End in the Village, singing his poems about war and loose women and nonconformity (I'd discovered his music in the Institute, and had played almost nothing else since), every New Yorker I knew was getting laid every night, and I'd heard they were smoking pot in the streets. Kentucky felt like a closet. I transferred to Columbia in September of 1966.

I WAS TWENTY-TWO THAT FALL. Most of my St. Paul's classmates had finished college three months before, were on their ways now into law school or graduate school or Vietnam, or the teaching jobs or Peace Corps rotations that would earn them deferrals from the draft. I was becoming more troubled by this, and would be more so as time went on: that I had dropped behind in the life-course sweepstakes that were only now beginning to seem important; that I was officially "unadaptable" for inclusion in what was fast becoming my generation's war.

It was still a distant war, but seeming closer with every morning's paper. There were 385,000 troops in Vietnam by the end of that year—1966—with 6,000 already dead; another 10,000 would die before the next year was out. There had been teach-ins already on some campuses, and 25,000 protesters at a march down Fifth

Avenue in the spring. William Fulbright had opened congressional hearings on the war; Bobby Kennedy had denounced it in a scathing speech on the Senate floor in January ("a road that leads to catastrophe for all mankind"); Martin Luther King, the following spring, would be preaching draft resistance, calling America "the greatest purveyor of violence in the world."

I was living off-campus in a five-floor walk-up on East Eighty-ninth Street, taking a bus and a subway up and back to the Columbia campus every day. I knew almost no one there and took no part at all in the life of the school. Sometimes, in my first months in New York, I'd stay uptown after classes and eat a burger-and-beer supper at the Gold Rail on Broadway, where I'd be surrounded by students I didn't know talking about parties I hadn't been to or plans for a rally over some campus grievance I'd never heard about. I felt misplaced and adrift—as I had at St. Paul's and Centre—though the reasons felt different now.

I don't remember much else about that year. The big-city fantasies never came to fruition—never even came close. I was lonely. I wrote my papers and read my assignments; I went to classes, spent a lot of time in bars, where sometimes I met women—it was the time in my life, that year and the year after, when "girls" were starting to be "women" and sex was becoming more expectation than prize. Often on weekends, I would go to my uncle's in Connecticut, where I would drink too much bourbon, watch *Gunsmoke* with my aunt Peggy—or with one of my cousins, Stuart or Sandy, if either one were home—or shoot pool in town with an old family retainer named Harold, who was crusty and wonderful and used to tell stories of his youth spent in pool halls and freight yards and other seedy, broken-down, full-of-life venues I always thrilled to hear about.

Everything seemed to be happening somewhere else. Or to someone else. Or it had happened before I got there—or even before I was *born*. I was looking for something I wasn't finding—I knew that much. I wasn't finding it at Columbia, which seemed as alien to me as Centre had, though I couldn't have told you why. My Tuxedo Park friends were gone now from my life, part of a world that had ended like stopped music the day my father died. The war wouldn't take me—I didn't even feel I'd earned the right to *talk* about it, at least not with those who knew my status. My uncle, whom I liked but still scarcely knew, treated me with a solicitude so abounding I sometimes felt the urge to smash plates against the wall.

More and more now, I was spending my time alone: reading dark, brooding, existential novels; drinking in bars with strangers, then later—and increasingly, as the months passed—cutting classes to go to the track. I would begin in the afternoons at Belmont or Aqueduct, and after that, if there was anything still left in my wallet, take the three-dollar limo to Yonkers or Roosevelt to bet on the trotters at night. When I lost, I pawned or borrowed—and at one point, scammed more than $1,000 in a phony traveler's-check loss. When I won, more and more often I'd take a taxi from the trotters to LaGuardia Airport, catch the 11:59 P.M. Eastern Airlines flight to San Juan, and play blackjack at the La Concha Hotel-Casino for as long as I could support myself there. And at least once a week, sometimes two or three nights running, I played with my friend Stanley in a high-low stud game with the policemen and zoo workers in a storage locker behind the monkey cages in Central Park.

Meanwhile, amazingly, I was trying to write. Short stories mostly, sometimes essays, once even a play. None of it ventured far from home—one story was a dreamy update of Dostoyevsky's *The Gambler;* the play was set in a New England mental hospital—and none of it, except for posterity, is worth the time to read today. But there was an honesty to it. I wrote mostly about questing, rudderless young people trying to find their balance in all the wrong ways: gambling, nomadic travels, serial seductions, even murder. I wrote a long essay about the Nebraska oil fields, another about the monastery in Big Sur. I hung around the bookstore in the Scribner's Building on Fifth Avenue, browsing fiction by newly launched young authors, sampling styles, reading dust-cover bios for accounts of troubled early lives.

AT AROUND FOUR O'CLOCK ONE MORNING in February or March of 1968, I was on my way back from the Central Park poker game. I had lost, badly, probably for the third or fourth night in a row. I was tired—I hadn't slept in two days—worried sick about the debt-hole I was digging myself into over poker and the horses, and just generally depressed about life. I would be staying that night with Stanley, sleeping on a couch in his family's apartment in the U.N. Plaza on East Forty-ninth Street. I owed Stanley money. I owed money to half the people I knew.

We were in the elevator in the lobby, just Stanley and I, waiting for the elevator door to close, when another man got in. It was Bobby Kennedy. He was alone. He looked tired—more tired than I was, exhausted. His suit was rumpled and he had gray bags under his eyes. He was carrying a copy of the *New York Times*. There was a story about him on the front page, which he was trying to read. It was around that time—the middle of March—that he announced his candidacy for the Democratic nomination, so the story may have been about that; I don't remember. He looked up from his paper, smiled, and said, "Good morning, boys." I said, "Good morning, Senator." He got off before we did. I never saw him again except on television, and had never seen him before—though he'd been a hero to me since his first days in the Senate. He died the sixth of June.

That was the end of something for me. The two of us, the senator and I, both on that elevator on our way up to bed, both young and smart and educated and with gifts, worn out for such contrary reasons. He won crowds with talk of "moral leadership for the planet"; I woke up every morning to the *Daily Racing Form*. It made me sick to think about. I never played again in that game in the zoo, or ever again with Stanley. The track remained a seduction, but with a sour taste now that hadn't been there before. Something important had happened, and I knew it, though it would be a long time taking full shape.

This was the spring of the Tet Offensive, the most vicious three months of the war. It was the spring that John Cocroft, drunk and embittered on his sandbags in Vung Tau, would begin down the path that would leave him cursing himself and his country, with sixty stitches in his head. And that Peter Johnson, with the Army Special Forces, would die in an assault near Qui Nhon; and John Kerry, by then a navy lieutenant crossing the Pacific bound for the Gulf of Tonkin, would be handed a telegram that would tell him that his best friend had been killed by a rocket-propelled grenade. ("I am empty, bitter, angry and desperately lost," he would write home, "with nothing but war, violence and more war around me. I just don't believe it was meant to be this cruel and senseless . . . Why?")

IT WAS AN AMAZING TIME. Every day brought some new madness. Martin Luther King was murdered in April. Two weeks later, I stood in a crowd with a thousand others outside Low Library at Columbia, smoking joints and cheering while strangers threw bagfuls of sandwiches through the open windows to the student occupiers inside—a day before the police came and dragged them out by their hair. Six weeks after that Bobby Kennedy was murdered in California, and I lay on the couch of my girlfriend's apartment and swore and ranted and cried at the TV till we both fell asleep in front of it.

All that spring and summer, the nation's black ghettos burned and rioted: Cleveland, Chicago, Washington, Newark, Los Angeles, New York. It was the year of the Poor People's March on Washington and Eugene McCarthy's "Children's Crusade"; the year three Black Panthers were shot to death by police in Los Angeles while another one ran for president. The Beatles went to India that year; Jerry Rubin went to the Capitol dressed in a Viet Cong flag, John and Yoko got naked for the cameras. In Central Park, a ninety-two-year-old woman, a Quaker, set herself on fire. At the end of August, at the Democratic Convention in Chicago, twelve thousand police and National Guardsmen beat heads on national TV. If you'd watched the six o'clock news every night but otherwise lived in a closet, you'd have sworn the world had gone mad.

To be twenty-three or twenty-four and living at the center of all this, you could get lost before you even saw the perils. Lots of people did. I did more than most. There were so many seductions. An unjust war, a government that lied about it, racial injustice, murdered martyrs, inequities everywhere you looked. And *so many of us*—hundreds of thousands, millions even. It felt almost like an army. And we had our icons. Tom Hayden, Mark

Rudd, Bobby Seale, Cleaver, King, Kennedy, McCarthy, Che, many more. And the music. We had Dylan and Baez and "Hey Jude" and "Abraham, Martin and John," songs you could dream with and songs you could shout—"ONE-TWO-THREE, WHAT'RE WE *FIGHTIN'* FOR? DON'T ASK ME, I DON'T GIVE A DAMN! NEXT STOP IS *VI-ET-NAM* . . ." And everybody was getting nude and making love in strawberry fields and smoking Hawaiian dope. It was mad and it was wonderful. But it had tipped me over like a bathtub toy in a storm.

It's easy to see now, looking back. There was no ballast, no rudder, nothing to root me or hold me steady or send me straight instead of left. My parents were dead, had never been there to begin with—the only real structure I'd known, from ten years old, had been at boarding schools. My aunt and uncle were kind, wise, and well-meaning, but I was a nephew to them. They opened their home to me, advised me when I asked them, protected what they could of my interests. They did what they could do.

And I did what I was bound to—I went where the pull was strongest. And in New York and at Columbia in the late 1960s, the pull was away from the center. Away from everything entrenched or endowed with authority; away from structure, tradition, ritual, precedent, reward-and-punishment, deference to elderly thought. Which was most of what I knew.

When you're brought up, as I was—at home and in my early school years, but nowhere more than at St.

Paul's—to measure yourself in acts of compliance and to revere what went before, then suddenly the rules are trashed and the old models thrown over, the way is laid for anarchy. Especially if there's no sense that the world will be fair—and there was none of that with me. The world had always seemed unfair. Now it was being turned on its end. There didn't seem any good reason to do—or not to do—anything at all.

SOMETIME EARLY IN THE SUMMER OF 1968, I must have gotten a letter from Columbia informing me that I'd been dropped. I don't remember that. The first I remember is sitting in the office of a plump, oily-faced dean named Fuss on August 21 or 22—the Soviets had invaded Czechoslovakia a day or two before—begging him to reconsider my dismissal. He was unmoved. I left, and spent the rest of that afternoon and evening on the couch of my cousin's wife, Lucy, crying and talking and watching Brezhnev's tanks roll through the streets of Prague, and—later, for I was there many hours—playing Battleship and drinking bourbon until we were both too exhausted to talk. I left there with an understanding I don't think I'd ever had before: that there is an allotment of failures in any life before the life itself becomes a failed one, and that I was getting close to mine.

There were other lessons, other moments that wouldn't go away. One came at around the same time, on a weekend morning in the summer of 1968 or '69—it could have been either one—when I woke up at my uncle's in Connecticut. It was June, I think; I hadn't been there in months. My cousins were home from work or college; we were going to play tennis and swim. I went downstairs for breakfast; the front page of the morning paper showed a large photo of a protester, dirty-looking and naked to the waist, waving a burning American flag. My uncle, whom I knew to be a temperate man, sometimes somber, other times with a twinkle but always coolheaded in his ways, was sitting at the dining-room table, red-eyed, shaking his head and talking to himself: "*How can they do that? How can they do that*?" he kept asking. He was incensed, unbalanced, almost beside himself. I'd never seen him that way.

I was fond of my uncle Jack. I respected him. He had founded a company, an aluminum mill in Connecticut, had run it for thirty years as it grew to ten or twelve times its original size. He went to his employees' weddings and birthdays, hosted barbecues every year for the workers in his plant. During the war, he'd been a dollar-a-year man, and kept the letter from FDR in a black plastic frame on the wall of his study at home. He gave away lots of money, served on a lot of company boards; at Christmas every year, the cards that came, hung on strings across a bookcase in the living room, ran the width of the room from the bottom shelf nearly to the ceiling.

And he believed in America. I knew this about him, knew it without question, though I wouldn't have put it that way then.

So to see him so shaken by that photo, so utterly undone—it seemed a kind of desecration. And to know that the hurt had been done by someone not unlike me, someone young and angry and moved by many of the same things: I felt a shame that morning, sitting across from him in his dining room eating my eggs and toast, that I wouldn't have thought possible before. Some of the romance of what we all were living, some of the exhilaration I'd been carrying around the last two years, went out of things for me that day. And some of it never came back.

IN FEBRUARY 1969, I ENROLLED AT my third college: the State University of New York at Stony Brook, on Long Island, an hour east of the city. I was nearly twenty-five. For the next sixteen months—until I graduated, in June a year later—I would stay away from friends' and family parties for fear someone would ask what I was doing with my life. I was ashamed.

I could write a whole book about 1969 (I've actually thought hard about it), but in another sense, a more personal sense, there isn't that much to say. It was a seismic year for the country. It was the year of Woodstock and the first moon landing, the year 250,000 marched on Washington and two dozen college campuses exploded in open rage. In Vietnam, the war peaked that year—with 540,000 troops—and the first drawdowns began. On Christopher Street in New York, a block from where I was living, a police raid on a gay bar at the end of June set off the riots that would mark the start of gay liberation. It was the year the country did its very worst bleeding, but also began to heal.

For me though, all this seemed suddenly in the background. I cared about it still; still felt anger at the injustices, some of the same sweetness at the little victories. But it was different now; it had been different since my ten minutes in Dean Fuss's office and the long afternoon on Lucy's couch in June. I was afraid now. I had seen myself: the quester after empty moments of aliveness, the pinball caroming. And it had frightened me.

(One time especially. An afternoon the autumn before, not long after the Columbia debacle, riding back from the racetrack with three or four slack-faced old regulars in a broken-down Cadillac—they called them "limos" and charged three dollars a head. The old guys were sitting on every side of me—right, left, and front—reeking of beer and sweat, talking across me, all at once, about the "lousy, fuckin' exacta in the fifth" and how Baez had "fuckin' kicked the seventh," just like he'd done in some other race they all recalled a week or a month or six months before. They were old, these men, probably sixty or more, and ratty-looking and smelly and foul-mouthed and brimming over with losers' memories. And one second they were talking across me, fouling the air, filling the old car with their dolor, fueling my contempt—and the next second *they were me.* It was very real. I got out at the first stop in Manhattan, walked home in a sweat, and didn't go back to the track again the rest of my time in New York.)

All that spring and the following fall and winter, three or four days a week, I commuted from my apartment on Tenth Street, sometimes on the Long Island Rail Road, other times in my gray '67 Camaro, to the Stony Brook campus for classes. I stopped the poker games along with the racetrack; I cut back on the drinking—though I never came close to stopping—and kept myself mostly out of bars. At home in the evenings, I read and wrote my assignments, then went to bed in time to start again. One day in my second semester—the fall of '69—I went uptown to the ASPCA on Ninety-second Street, where I found an ugly little blond puppy-mutt in a cage with a date on it that told me her time was nearly up. I claimed her and named her Phoebe, and found in myself a devotion, and a capacity for caring, I hadn't known was there.

WHEN I TRY TO GO BACK and touch the pulse of that young man, driven through those months by his sudden, overdue rush to become, I'm almost overwhelmed by the memory I have of feeling lost: literally lost, grabbing on to whatever seemed warm or hopeful or familiar—schooldays, early bedtimes, a new puppy—acting mostly out of need and panic and will. I'd never owned much of a compass to begin with—alcoholic families are like that, and mine had fractured earlier than most. But there had always at least been Authority: my father, the schoolmasters, the system, someone or something to set the standards, someone to fear if not to obey. And all that now seemed gone.

And there had been something else, too, that was gone now, something even more central. There had been the sense, reinforced in a hundred ways—especially at St. Paul's—that the world was a certain kind of place. It was a place of endless promise for those who cared to sweat for it, a place where character counted for more than fate or luck. It was a world that rewarded manliness, restraint, civility (which could also be read as breeding), charity, adherence to tradition, and fair play. There was no place in it for mushy thinking, or for laziness, cowardice, moral weakness, or emotions not properly reined in. It was a world built on certain assumptions of order. A more-or-less morally static, meritocratic world.

But no longer. Now we were burning flags in public parks, building bonfires of our draft cards, running off to Canada to escape a duty our fathers had loved to brag about. Everybody was getting high and getting laid—it was almost too easy to be fun—the cops were pigs, the president was a liar, the "homos" were marching on Washington. And on and on and on. There were no assumptions anymore. And sometimes, to me anyway, it felt a lot more like chaos than change.

When you're lost, you seek out the familiar. I began spending more weekends in Connecticut: reading, playing tennis, playing board games with my cousins or pick-up hockey at a pond a mile from the house. Early that same spring, the spring of 1969, I adopted the New York Mets—fell in love with them, became an overnight fanatic—and made a $10 bet with my cousin Stuart, at thirty-to-one odds, that they would win the World Series that year. (They were a miserable team, had finished ninth in their division the season before, twenty-four games off the lead. They had no chance, none at all, they were hopeless—which was most of why I loved them.) All season long I followed them, made them mine so completely I'd almost cry when they lost.

And they felt it—they heard me. On September 5, a month from the end of the season, they were in second place, five games behind Chicago. They split a double-header that day, against Philadelphia, then won twenty-two of their last twenty-seven, to win the pennant going away. Two weeks later they beat Baltimore, four games to one, to win the World Series. Under the tree that Christmas, there was an envelope for Stuart, letting him off most of the $300 he wasn't making enough to afford:

Oh Stu, are you yet a believer
In the arm of Met pitcher Tom Seaver?
Has the bat of Agee yet caused you to see
that the Mets are a costly deceiver? . . .

It was that July, midway through the Mets' season (they were in second place at the time, and would stay there till September), that I read about the Appalachia offer. I'd turned twenty-five a day or two before, had finished my first semester at Stony Brook with all A's, and was half in love with my advisor there, Rose Zimbardo, who was trying to make me see that there was more to life than the language that describes it and more to written language than lushness. I was coming to understand that. I was coming to understand that a telegram to the head of the Senate Foreign Relations Committee—William Fulbright—had more chance of making a difference than a "PEACE NOW!" placard on the shoulder of a marcher in Bryant Park. I was reading less and less of the novels of Golding and Vonnegut and more of the columns of the *New York Post*'s Pete Hamill, whose coarse, angry prose and underdog sympathies were becoming a model for me.

I'd grown distrustful of abstractions, of easy inspiration, the mushy thinking that burned flags and bras and draft cards in the name of change that never seemed to come. There was something in me now that wanted reason and order and hard thinking—but still wanted the world to be fair.

I left for West Virginia the second week of July. I returned five weeks later with a sadness and anger I almost didn't recognize at first, and a far keener sense of what really might matter to me. All that fall and winter, in a frenzy I can still almost summon, I came and went from Stony Brook, did the coursework that needed to be done, and wrote and rewrote the drafts of the piece the *Louisville Courier-Journal* Sunday editor had told me, more than once, the paper couldn't use. But I knew that they *could* use it and that they would use it; I knew it in a way you can only know such things at a certain early time in your life.

In April 1970 they published the article ("Enough Nonsense about Appalachia") in a five-page spread that led with a photo of me chucking the chin of Sally Robinette's three-month-old baby girl. ("The author with his hostess and a young member of the family.") A month later I graduated with honors from Stony Brook. A week or so after that I went with my girlfriend, Gabriella, my dark-haired old love from Centre who was back again in my life, to a used-car lot in New Jersey, where we bought the '65 van that would take us to Oregon and back.

We left the next morning—by the southern route, through Tennessee and the Texas Panhandle—with two air mattresses in back and Phoebe between us on her belly, paws under her chin, on the raised gray engine-housing console that sat like someone's old trunk across half of the front of the van. We were gone six weeks. The high point of the trip—probably of our three or four years together, which were nearly at an end—was a week in a cabin outside Eureka on U.S. 101, living on fried eggs and steamed clams, reading *Lolita,* gawking at the redwoods, and listening to the seals at night.

The Artist Soldier

Most of the masters' wives are ugly, at least the ones who come to the dining hall with their husbands. A lot of them are old and saggy and tired-looking, like if you left them alone for five minutes they could go to sleep in their seats. A few of them are fat—and a lot of the skinny ones, especially the younger ones, look like boys with dresses on.

But Mrs. Marcy is sexy. Pretty too, but really sexy—no other wife, in my opinion, even comes close. She has dark eyes and straight, dark hair that she has to keep brushing back from her face; and she's thin in the good way, like some models, with little coffee-cup boobs that you can just barely see sort of dipping under her blouse. And she has this incredible smile—and this way of looking at you when you're talking like she thinks you're the coolest person in the world.

She wears dark red lipstick, which is always fresh when she comes to the table. Then right at the end, just before she gets up to leave with her husband, she always pulls out her lipstick and this little mirror she carries, and freshens it again. (I love to watch her do this: pull her lips back tight against her teeth, then pucker them again at the end. I'm not the only one who watches—I think she knows it, too.) Then she blots it very carefully with a napkin, always in just the same way, folds the napkin in two and leaves it at her place.

I have to be careful how I do this. It used to be easy, when I was on waiter duty at the Marcys' table—I would just take the napkin off the tray on my way out to the kitchen and put it in my pocket. Now I'm at Mr. Archer's table all the way on the other side of the dining hall, and it's harder to get over there and not be noticed before the napkin gets cleared away.

But usually I can. And I'll get the napkin and keep it in my pocket, or sometimes inside of a book, until I'm alone in my room at night. Then I'll close the door, take it out and unfold it, kind of rub my face in it a little to get the smell, then press my lips over Mrs. Marcy's lip print—which is always red and perfect, with all the little lines where the veins are—and pretend I'm kissing her. And I will be hard, and my hand will be there. And then sometimes I will do it again.

If anybody found out they would call me a homo—you are a homo if you do anything that isn't actually with a girl. Last year in second form I was a homo. A bunch of us last year were homos: in the Lower School study hall bathroom, or sometimes in our alcoves on weekend afternoons, beating each other off. For me, it was partly a way of getting the Regs to like me—a lot of them were homos that year, too. But then after the year ended and we came back in September, it was like it had never happened. Nobody ever talked about it. The Regs didn't like me. There were no homos anymore.

So now I take Mrs. Marcy to my room at night—which I like better anyway. And when I see her the next morning in the dining hall, talking at the table with the boys and her husband like nothing had happened, I stop feeling funny or guilty. And I want to kiss her again.

OF THE TWENTY-TWO BOYS IN THE front row of that 1958 photo—the only ones whose bottom halves you can see—all but two stand more or less erect, feet close together, eyes forward toward the camera. The two exceptions are in identical poses: both vaguely sneering, both with legs spread wide, hips forward, shoulders back. Gunslinger poses. Two young kids with something to prove. I am one of them. The other is Chad Floyd.

"I was a pretender there," Chad writes me in an email today. "I didn't feel a part of that world at all. I was never particularly bothered that I didn't, but I didn't. It was amazing though, arriving at breakfast in Hargate at seven in the morning, alongside a bunch of thirteen-year-olds in three-piece suits with gold watches and chains. I'd be in this sleepy haze, just trying to get my tie knotted, and here would be the Regs, walking serenely, not a care in the world, decked out in tailored suits with vests, regimental ties all perfectly knotted, and—honest to God—one kid with a watch chain dangling out of his vest. I just wasn't prepared for that stuff."

He was from Washington—Georgetown—the only child of a socialite mother and a civil-service father who could trace his lineage back to a homestead in Jamestown in 1621. An ancestor had signed the Declaration of Independence; another had died (probably of appendicitis) on his way west with Lewis and Clark. Chad spent as much time as some of the rest of us, as a child, passing hors d'oeuvres at his parents' parties—"politicians, diplomats, journalists, lobbyists and always the bridge players"—went to the best private school in Washington, to Miss Shippen's Dancing School at ten, spent his summers in Vermont, New Hampshire, Rehoboth Beach, and Cape May.

"Our little house in Georgetown was often filled with D.C. society," he will write me in an email after our first meeting—then will add, almost as an afterthought: "and alcoholism was always a problem, especially for my father, whose job required that he entertain and be entertained more or less nonstop."

When I ask him later, both in person and in my own

emails, for his thoughts on his father's drinking, he explains it first mostly as a function of time and place ("Washington is a hard-drinking town . . . Dad's job put him in the thick of it"), then seems to concede that it might have been more serious than that: "The alcohol poisoned him. He got very sick from it when I was quite young—say, up to my fifth year. Then he went on the wagon for many years. . . ."

Still, for all the common threads that linked us, he wasn't a legacy student (his father had met the school's sixth rector, Henry Kittredge, at a cocktail party in the late 1940s and decided on the spot that St. Paul's would be the school for his son); he wasn't from Greenwich or Long Island or the Upper East Side or any of the other northeastern old-money enclaves that informed the ethos of the Regs. He dressed wrong, he wore his hair in a buzz cut. He may have talked a little Southern. Any one of those, and a hundred other things, would have made you a pretender back then.

I remember Chad well. Short and skinny, one of the smallest in the class, he wore khakis everywhere, drummed his fingers constantly on tabletops, was always in a hurry, walked and talked a little too fast. He seemed young to me—scrawny, vulnerable, underdeveloped. Apparently also to himself: "I had a sense of being less mature," he says today. "There were guys already shaving."

I had the same problem. I dreaded going in the shower, would check for pubic hair once or twice a day. And *I* was short and skinny, too, until I grew six inches between fourth- and fifth-form years. And we knew some of the same girls, New York girls who went to school in the South—one I was madly in love with and would invite for Dance Weekend fifth-form year, another I didn't think much of at the time but would marry fifteen years later.

So we had those things in common. Along with the sense of being out of step. I liked Chad. We were never close—I was never close to anyone at St. Paul's—but we talked sometimes, came and went from classes together, played milk-carton hockey in the hallways of Manville, where we both lived fourth-form year. There was a natural connection there. (He must have thought so, too, and for some of the same reasons: "I felt an affinity toward you because you and I were about the same size," he wrote in an email forty-six years later. "And we were similarly immature physically . . . and had a lot of energy, and were a little casual about schoolwork.")

The difference was, he never seemed to care about any of it. His scrawniness, his youth, his outsider status—he never seemed troubled by anything at all, while I was tortured constantly, lay awake nights inventing lines to get Mary or Maggie up for Dance Weekend, spent half my vacations in Brooks Brothers poring over which loafers, shirts, and tie pins would pass muster with the Regs.

I see today what made us different, though it was probably beyond me then. He didn't care because it wasn't his world; he didn't come from it, didn't belong to it, it held no thrall for him: "It was fascinating, I guess, in a naive sort of way," he wrote me in an email. "In the end, I think, I liked being from Washington rather than from New York or Philadelphia. [I liked] being an outsider at the school."

There were others in the form like Chad, of course, boys who didn't fit and didn't care, or who fit just fine but didn't care anyway, weren't drawn by the lure of French cuffs and gold watch chains at seven in the morning. One of these was Bill Tilghman (then known as Forbes), a pale, thin, shy-seeming, old-moneyed Boston boy with all the legacy credentials—grandfather, father, cousins, and brother—but more interest in playing the trumpet than in anything the Regs had to offer. Chad's drums and Bill's trumpet found each other early. That, along with a mutual nuttiness ("Our real bond was humor," Bill tells me. "We laughed more than we talked."), rooted a friendship that began their first week as third-formers and is now going on fifty years old. Today they are godfathers to each other's children, were best men in each other's weddings, and speak of one another with an unafraid familiarity that is rare and warming to see.

"My friendship with Bill was the key to my time at St. Paul's," Chad would tell me the first day we met. "It insulated me, it gave me a sort of cover, I think, from all that stuff that went on with the Regs and the jocks."

I HADN'T SEEN HIM IN NEARLY forty years, since the wedding of a mutual friend (the same girl I'd asked to

Dance Weekend at St. Paul's) in Connecticut in the late sixties, where the bride and groom, who would be divorced three years later, had been married in a wooded grotto, then departed the party in a hot-air balloon. We were sitting now at a table by the window in a restaurant in Hanover, New Hampshire, where Chad, who is a founding partner in an architecture firm, had just finished an appointment at Dartmouth College, a longtime client of the firm.

He looked nothing like I remembered him. No longer scrawny or skittish, he is bald now, very trim and solid-seeming, and was wearing a blue blazer, pale shirt, and rust-colored, sharply pressed corduroy trousers. There was nothing about him that would tell you he'd had an uncertain moment in his life.

He looks about his age—sixty-two, the same as all of us, give or take a year—but gives off a wholesomeness that could cause you to misjudge. He sits straight, speaks softly, and chooses his words with great care—and seems very certain once he speaks them. For all that, though, there is a warmth about him, a humility almost, that belies all that certainty. I have the thought at one point: he must be very, very good at winning clients.

We talk for the first little while about Bill and their friendship, about their shared interest in jazz and the music they used to like to play. ("Dave Brubeck or Miles Davis, with me on the drums and him on the trumpet or bass.") Then he switches the subject to drama, his other big interest at St. Paul's; he asks if I remember a performance of

The Caine Mutiny Court-Martial, where he played the part of a courtroom witness and John Kerry was Captain Queeg. I say that I don't remember, that it may have been sixth-form year, the year after I was gone. "Kerry was a good Queeg," he says. "He really got into that role."

A word or two on that, and we're back to music again—it seems always on the outskirts of his thoughts. He remembers another school production he was part of: this one with another friend, also a guest at that long-ago Connecticut wedding. "He had a really hip technique on the piano," Chad remembers. Then he tells the story of how the two of them hooked up fourth-form year in a drums-piano duo to win second prize in the school's yearly talent show:

"We played 'Lullaby of Birdland' and 'The Lady Is a Tramp.' I had about a 102 fever and had to talk my way out of the cooler for the event. But what really put us over the top was Ralph Peer [another classmate], a real techy kind of guy, a guy with keys always hanging off his belt. He agreed to dim the colored strip-lights on the stage back and forth real slowly while we played, so the red would turn to purple, then purple to blue, blue to green, and so on. That was pretty revolutionary at St. Paul's in 1959. They kind of had to recognize us."

He could talk all day about his music. He is still a drummer, plays in an eight-piece jazz band, the Essex Corinthian Jazz Band, every Wednesday night eight months a year, at a little seafood place on the waterfront near his home in Connecticut: "a sawdust-on-the-floor kind of place," he has told me in an email. "We have fans who come every Wednesday. People dance, get drunk, behave in ways they probably regret the next day."

The next time we meet, he will come with photos, including one or two of the band, and I can see in them the plain good fun he speaks of: there on the stage, straddling the drum set, eyes half-closed, lips pursed, bald head glowing—he seems nothing at all like the man across from me in the blue blazer, cell phone jangling every three or four minutes on his hip, choosing his words so carefully. Much more the twitchy, fast-talking, skinny little khakied kid I knew.

IN THE GEORGETOWN NEIGHBORHOOD where he grew up, there was a black Baptist church five doors down from his home. He used to go there sometimes on Sundays, with his black neighbor-friend Peebles, having just returned with his parents from the suit-and-tie Episcopal service three blocks away, where he served as an altar boy.

"That little church rocked," he tells me. "I loved hearing the music that flowed from those tall windows on hot Sundays, and those red choir robes they had all swaying, and the smiling, the togetherness of it all. I felt a real connection there, to the music and to the people inside."

A well brought-up, 1950s white boy from the city, ten or twelve years old, scrubbed clean and in his Sunday best, dropping by a black church to take in some gospel hymns. It's quite an image—it makes me smile just to think about—though it took me our first two meetings, with a long email in between, before I began to understand that its importance to Chad, at least today, has less to do with the music itself and more to do with its origins: why people sing to begin with, the emotions that link them, the bond that music inspires. It is what he likes to call the "connection to our collective soul."

It's less high-minded than it sounds. What he's really talking about is *tradition*. The longer you talk with him—no matter what the subject—the more the word comes up: the tradition of black Baptist music and its roots in soul and jazz ("great empathy music"), the "tension" in architecture "between tradition and innovation," the traditions of the old waterfront town where he lives—"old wooden boats, steam railroads, traditional Dixieland jazz." An essay he read in college by T. S. Eliot, "Tradition and the Individual Talent," which he mentions several times in a single conversation: "It opened my eyes to things—it calls for poetic connections to past works, even very difficult, hard-to-understand connections, as the key to great, enduring art."

It's hard to know where all this got its start. Maybe as early as the Baptist church in Georgetown; or not till later, when he learned from his father about his Jamestown ancestor Nathaniel Floyd and the other Floyd forebears who signed the Declaration, served under George Washington, or went west with Lewis and Clark. Wherever it started, it's pretty clear that it was deepened by the four years he spent at St. Paul's.

"I liked being at a place that went back a century and had a history," he would write me in an email after our first two meetings in New Hampshire. "I liked the idea of being at a school that was arguably the best or among the best in the country, and being part of a tradition there. The school expanded my world."

Then came Yale—which, to hear him describe it, was an almost seamless extension of St. Paul's. Bill Tilghman was there (the two were roommates, along with another St. Paul's alum); there were plays with the Drama Club—*Romeo and Juliet,* Sartre's *Men Without Shadows*—several set-design jobs that would plant the architecture seed, an English major that would veer toward the Victorian poets, drum-piano duos several times a month in the common room of Calhoun College. "We had motorcycles, and rented a little beach house in Guilford on weekends for $55 a month. My time at Yale was fantastic."

It was 1966. The war was still young, still building; by year's end there would be 385,000 U.S. troops in Vietnam. There were protests: 25,000 at the one on Fifth Avenue that May, but a month later, the same month Chad got his Yale diploma, NYU gave an honorary degree to Robert McNamara—unthinkable even a year later—and only about two hundred students walked out.

"There was some Green Beret guy going around the college circuit giving antiwar lectures," Chad remembers, "but I never paid much attention."

He believed in the war, or at least in the idea of service. "I was young," he says, "I was patriotic. And James

Bond films were a big thing back then." He had no real interest in graduate school (the main route to deferment) but felt relatively certain, if he waited to be drafted, he'd end up somewhere as a clerk: "because I'd been an English major and could type." He didn't want that. He wanted to be at the center of things—"and Vietnam was the center of the world at the time."

So, one day that spring of 1966, at about the same time John Kerry, also at Yale, was signing his navy enlistment papers, Chad and a roommate, Rick Beinecke, "walked down together to visit Colonel Stein"—the Marine Corps recruiter at Yale—"and he signed us up and gave us the test." Five months later he reported for duty at the Marine Officer Candidates School, Quantico, Virginia.

THERE IS A DIFFERENCE BETWEEN the way he talks about the marines—about *anything* involving the marines, even indirectly, including the war, the antiwar movement, his time in Vietnam—and the way he talks about other parts and periods of his life. His normal carefulness seems doubled now; he is quieter, more reflective, less inclined to levity. There is a soberness that surrounds the subject, a reverence almost, that comes across in his tone, his volume, the choice and pacing of his words. It is an odd thing when the subject changes: you find yourself slowing your *own* words, tempering your speech patterns, to more closely adjust to his.

A big part of this goes back to that same tradition

thing. There may be nothing, in Chad's world order, more suffused with tradition than the U.S. Marine Corps. He speaks often of the "esprit" that comes with service, refers to this or that former buddy as a "good marine," writes in an email of "the proud tradition that goes back to Iwo Jima, Belleau Wood and the Halls of Montezuma."

His politics are Republican. ("We ought to stay away from politics," he tells me five minutes into our first meeting.) He claims to have never had a drink in his life. He has such an aversion to dark corners that he once remarked to Bill Tilghman, whose home at the time was redolent with the strains of his parents' estrangement: "Let's forget all this heavy stuff and go somewhere and clown around." Yet he designs libraries for a living—describes himself as an artist—is attracted by complexities, reads the poetry of Eliot and Yeats.

He is a classic this way, a kind of archetype: the teetotaling jazz drummer, the stoical-yet-life-loving citizen-soldier, the humanist ex-marine, who might once have been played by Jimmy Stewart or Montgomery Clift. Or scripted by the Reverend Matthew Warren, our rector of forty-three years ago, if he'd ever been asked to sketch out his vision of the model product of his school.

THE SUMMER AFTER BOOT CAMP, on an island off the coast of Maine with Yale roommates Bill and Rick in attendance, Chad was married to his college girlfriend Julie, a marriage that wouldn't last his time away. ("We were too young and dumb to know better" is most of what he offers when I ask.) Three weeks later, in July 1967, he was flown to Da Nang, and from there to Cam Lo, on the DMZ between North and South Vietnam, where he was united with his first command, a sixty-man infantry platoon: "mostly blacks, known as 'splibs,' from Chicago, whites, called 'chucks,' from Appalachia, or Chicanos from LA. They were a tough bunch."

Three weeks after that, eight miles deep in the jungle on a hill overlooking the Ben Hai River, cut off from the main forces and out of radio contact, his platoon was ambushed by a unit of NVA—one member of which, appearing from behind vegetation with an AK-47 aimed at Chad, pulled the trigger from three feet away. And somehow missed. ("I was so shocked I just looked at the guy, didn't even take a shot back, though I was holding an M-16 I'd gotten off a dead marine. The marine behind me took care of him for me.")

There are several stories like this. He tells them, in person or by email, never without prompting, with the same flat thoroughness you might use to describe a traffic accident, some years later, to a judge.

Con Thien in September '67, a fire base his unit was assigned to reinforce: "It lasted three weeks. We couldn't send out patrols, couldn't even take a crap because they sighted their guns on the shitter whenever a guy went in." Bridge 28, outside Khe Sanh in April '68: "I was in charge of three platoons. The bridge had been secured by air cav—there was a squad on the bridge, we had to guard them. It was a big gun battle, lasted two nights, three days. It was pretty terrible. There was a book written about it if you're interested."

He is plainly uncomfortable on the subject of losses, will talk about them only in the most general terms: "Deaths and wounds of my troopers were tough to take. I worked hard to keep them safe. But certainly I lost some marines. Shit happens in combat. We all understood that. But I didn't come away from Vietnam with the feeling that people had died from my mistakes."

HE LEFT VIETNAM IN THE LATE summer of 1968, with two Bronze Stars and a Vietnamese Cross of Gallantry, just about the time that, bounced out of Columbia, I was coming apart on Lucy's couch in New York. John Cocroft by then was in a medical unit in Okinawa, being treated for the wrist he'd broken in his drunken rant in Vung Tau. John Kerry, one of those same nights, July 25, 1968, on leave between tours in Vietnam, was part of a crowd of forty-five thousand at Fenway Park in Boston—"the wildest night since the Red Sox won the pennant," a *Boston Globe* reporter wrote—watching Eugene McCarthy, a month before the Democratic Convention, deliver the most searing antiwar speech of his campaign.

The next stop for Chad was San Diego, where he would train recruits for the balance of his time. He'd been gone a year. The Tet Offensive by now was six months in the past; Kennedy and King had been murdered; McCarthy was drawing huge crowds. It was a far darker mood than he'd left.

"My hippie brother-in-law called me a baby-killer at the dinner table a week after I got back. I avoided wearing my uniform. No one, not even my parents' friends, ever showed the slightest appreciation—only relief I was back in one piece."

His thoughts on all this are not generous. The antiwar movement, as he sees it, was mostly the product of "a bunch of kids with too much entitlement, too much sense of their own power and importance, an overblown sense of the way things were going to be. I was a returning veteran, I'd been slogging through the mud the last year getting shot at, getting dysentery—at one point I was down to 112 pounds—and then I come home to *that* . . .

"So no, I didn't have much patience with it. It seemed self-serving to me, and totally futile. Kind of like Marlow"—in *Heart of Darkness*—"shooting off his cannon in the jungle. It didn't prove a thing."

And no, he says, he's experienced nothing like post-traumatic stress disorder—and doesn't have much sympathy with those who say they have.

"I left Vietnam without looking back. I don't understand people who, at sixty, define their lives in terms of an experience from thirty-five years ago, who can't shake the fact that they served in Vietnam and boy, was it a bitch. On the whole, this strikes me more as self-aggrandizement than emotional distress."

We've heard all this before: the angry veteran, lashing out at the hippie draft-resisters or at those who whine about psychic wounds. But coming from Chad, there's a strange sort of dissonance to it. His otherwise careful forbearance so at odds with his disdain; his attraction to ambiguity—Eliot, Sartre, Conrad—so completely belied by the flatness of his views on the war. At one point, sitting at a table over lunch in a Dartmouth College courtyard (it is our third meeting by now), he describes the sixties and early seventies as "an anomaly to the flow of our culture"—which he summarizes as "Hey, man, this is a gas, screw the system, let's go live in a commune somewhere." Then, not more than a minute later, he says this about the war: "It was oversimplified, grossly oversimplified by people who didn't understand it. And the simplifications have become an article of faith."

He seems deaf to his own duality. It's as if all that training and background—St. Paul's, Yale, all those years of steepage in civility and tolerance and intellectual rigor—had smashed up against something more elemental. And probably that's what it is. Chad was a skinny, skittish, unathletic boy, an only child of doting parents, aware at a young age, as he puts it, that "my life had been a protected one." The Marine Corps changed that, utterly. "I lived in the mud with my troops," he writes me in an email, "and came to know them like brothers. I was responsible for the lives of sixty people. I controlled tanks, jets, helicopters, men in life-and-death situations."

"It changed him," his old friend Bill will tell me

three months later over a dinner in Washington, D.C. "He was thirty pounds heavier, all muscle. He was different. He had a confidence I'd never seen before."

This is pretty classic stuff. About nest-leaving, manhood, rites of passage, self-actualization. Not to mention war. And for Chad, from all I can tell, it's the realest thing in the world, even today—for *all* his talk about leaving without looking back. And faced with an assault, any kind of assault, on something so real and dear and hard-won, it's not hard to see how all that forbearance, all that well-learned spacious thinking, could give out like an overworked muscle, too hard and tight to bend.

"The way things were for us," he says to me that same afternoon in the Dartmouth courtyard, in the course of an exchange of St. Paul's memories, "it was clear there were certain expectations, certain assumptions—sometimes stated, sometimes not, but you always knew they were there—about the way things were going to unfold . . .

"Then everything got turned upside-down, didn't it? Nothing really happened like that at all."

IT HAS BEEN AN UP-AND-DOWN ROAD for Chad. He lives today in a 3,600-square-foot house of his own design, with a view of salt marshes and distant hills, on a one-acre waterfront site in Essex, Connecticut. In the pictures I've seen of it—as a showpiece home in the display book for Centrebrook Architects, the firm he founded and helps run—it seems both rustic and majestic: weathered clapboard with a long, sloped roof wrapped by a gleaming white two-story deck, seeming to grow out of the marshes that surround it.

"It's a glory," he tells me, "but the pain was too great, and I guess I wish we'd just bought a nice little house and moved in."

The pain he is talking about is the pain his marriage has become. Brenda Floyd, over the last three years, has fallen into a deep and so far irreversible depression. She is housebound; she's not improving. The therapy and medications have been constant, but so far have done almost no good. For the first year the doctors believed the cause was a childhood head trauma. Since then it has been blamed on menopause, Lyme disease, fibromyalgia. Now no one any longer even pretends to be sure. And all this is unfolding with a thirteen-year-old in the house.

"It's been awful. It's been unrelenting. She can't be alone, she can't be with others, she can't be trusted by herself. And it's been incredibly tough on Logan. But he's strong. He's holding up."

He seems beleaguered. Every time we've met or written each other, over intervals of three months or so stretched over nearly two years, the prognosis for Brenda seems to have worsened just slightly; the horizon for improvement to have been stretched farther out. Always there seems to be some new doctor, some new time line or possible diagnosis, some medication that just failed and another about to receive the new investment of hope.

And all the while, in what could almost seem the second half of a parallel life, his architectural practice continues to soar. What started thirty years ago with four partners is now an eighty-person office with tens of millions of dollars in billings, commissions from cities, universities, museums, and major corporations, and buildings in twenty states. It is a very big name in the industry, as is Chad himself.

But it isn't easy getting him to take credit for this. Or even to concede that there is credit to take. Yes, he'll tell you, the company has prospered, and yes, it continues to grow: "But it's tougher all the time. We have to work our asses off to keep those good commissions coming . . . The pressure just doesn't let up. We're not the young hotspurs we were twenty-five years ago."

And what success he has enjoyed, he will write me in an email—in the same spare, efficient language he will use to describe his time in Vietnam—may not have been worth the price: "Brenda's condition has been challenged by the energy and intensity I've put into my career. This has been selfish of me."

Always with Chad, at every plane of his life, there is this press of personal responsibility: the selfishness he is guilty of, the weighty accountability for finding a better way ("I'm just trying to get her and us through this, and get her healthy again. The alternative is unthinkable."). And it hasn't only been Brenda. His father's drinking, he has told me, which had stopped for so many years during Chad's time at St. Paul's and Yale, began again when he was in Vietnam. This too, he says, can be traced to his own self-serving ways:

"I was an only child, and joining the marines was probably a thoughtless, selfish act, because it put terrible stress on my parents, who were very devoted to me. I got a letter in Vietnam from my father, promising me he'd quit again. And he did . . . And all these years I've never taken a drink."

Heavy burdens. And he's been a long time carrying them. It's hard not to wonder, thinking back to St. Paul's and Yale, where he came by the fortitude to resist all those early pressures, the debutante parties, the all-night college drunks, with nothing stronger than ginger ale; whether some of that tradition he holds so dear—the Christian forbearance, the rigorous thinking—might not have served him well, at sixteen or seventeen, when the gin and tonics were going around.

Certainly you can see the role the marines might have played in it all: that old Vietnam, "take that hill" approach to life, the full-speed-ahead frontal assault that allows for no defeat or compromise and exacts round-the-clock accountability.

You just hope, at some point along the line, there's some gentleness involved, some allowance made for frailty.

MEANWHILE, ALWAYS, HE HAS HIS MUSIC. It's hard to imagine, given what's going on with the rest of his life, where he would be without it. When he talks about his

Wednesday night gig at the seafood place, or his summer-only one at the yacht club in town ("a quieter crowd, and more sparse, so we use it partly for practice")—both of them on the set of drums he got as a Christmas present from Brenda—everything else, for the moment, drops away. It's as though here alone, in this single corner of his troubled, sectioned life, there is allowance made for simplicity. And even here, only because it's part of something larger:

"It's an expression of culture. There's empathy in it. And tradition. Fun, empathy, tradition, all that—Cannonball Adderley, John Coltrane, Miles Davis, all those guys. They're at the center of my life."

Loving Widely

Mr. Honea is a minister. He is from Texas, and has a pale, red face and this slow sophisticated drawl. I like him. He smiles a lot—he is almost always smiling—and when he talks to you, no matter what he is saying, it almost never comes out harsh or angry. He is different from most of the other masters that way.

He is my fifth-form sacred studies teacher. Mostly what we do is read books and plays—last month we read Separate Tables*—then talk in class about what they have* *to say about man and God, or about ethics or morality. Sometimes we read the newspaper, or newsmagazines, like* Time *or* Life, *and try to do the same thing.*

Adolf Eichmann is on trial in Israel right now for what he did to the Jews in the war. Last week Mr. Honea told us that that would be our new assignment: to read everything we could about Eichmann and the trial, think about what we believed should be done to him—whether he should be put to death or not, and why—then come to class with our opinions.

I don't think he should be put to death. I think it seems kind of hypocritical—to punish murder with death—and I also think that, in some way, it would be a more fitting punishment for him to stay alive in jail. He would be a sort of living reminder.

Anyway, this was what I argued in class when Mr. Honea called on me last week. Two other boys also got called on. (You never know, the way he runs the class, when your turn is going to come.) Both said they thought that Eichmann should die, and gave their reasons for this. I didn't agree with them, but I thought their arguments were good—especially one, who talked about the bad effects of his being spared, especially on the Jews.

Once we had presented our arguments, Mr. Honea called for a vote. Only one other boy agreed with me—there were eleven votes for death.

For the rest of the class, about another half hour, we debated the issue some more, this time with everyone involved. More and more as I listened, I began to change my mind—not change my mind, really, so much as just give in.

The other arguments were all so similar, and made sense. And there were so many more of them.

About three minutes before the end, I raised my hand and said this. I said that I had changed my mind, that I had been persuaded by the majority that Eichmann deserved to die. I thought I might get some silent credit for this from Mr. Honea—for not being stubborn, for being willing to open my mind.

He smiled his little smile, and I thought that would be it. Then he asked me, very gently, if I still believed it was hypocritical to punish death with death. I said that I still did, but that the other factors now seemed stronger.

"Do you believe that Adolph Eichmann, right now in Jerusalem, is getting a fair trial?" he asked me then.

"Yes, I think he is. From what I can tell, he is."

"Why do you think so?"

I said something about the judges and the court, and the lawyers for both sides.

"Do you believe that most of the people there in court right now, privately, in their hearts, believe that Eichmann is guilty?"

I said that yes, I supposed they probably did.

"Well then," he said, his tone still kind, his smile still wide and gentle: "Why shouldn't his lawyers just sit down and shut up—the way you want to do now—and save everybody the trouble?"

Then he said that my assignment for the next class would be to further defend—both orally and in writing—my argument for sparing Eichmann. I could tell by the way he said this that he was not rebuking me: that he thought my opinion was worthwhile, and worthy of being defended. I worked hard between classes on the project; I think I did a good job.

At the end of class this week, there was another vote. Eichmann still got the death penalty (as he would, of course, in real life), but it was closer than before—four votes now went my way. I had changed three minds. I had changed three minds with my words.

I am still feeling the excitement from this. It's a kind I have never felt before.

MONSIEUR JACQUES, IF I REMEMBER RIGHT, was my fourth-form French teacher. I didn't like him. He frightened me. He was round and wispy-haired and florid; he said preposterous things and was prone to rapid, sometimes scary outbursts. He shot saliva when he talked. His accent was too French. I don't think he liked me either.

To Philip Heckscher he is immortal. He is the teacher whose old class notebooks he keeps stashed today in his bedroom, whose admonition about being kind to toll collectors—because "they are lonely in their little booths"—remains a kind of mantra thirty years after his death. He is the original model for "loving widely"—which is at the core of Philip's dealings with the world. He speaks of him as one might speak of a mentor or spiritual master. When he quotes him, which he does frequently, it is always with the accent intact.

"He told us once, '*You* could masturbate behind zee telephone pole. *I* could make love to zee wall.'" What he meant by this, Philip explains to me (I've had to ask for an explanation), is that "We were pitiful little adolescents—squirrel-brains—playing with our penises, while *he* could make love to the world."

This was a man, as Philip recalls him, who one day, with a wasp buzzing threateningly around his apartment, poured a saucer of milk for it to drink from. "He thought the wasp might be happier if he had some milk. He was an antidote to all that [St. Paul's] coldness. He was spiritual, he was emotional, he was personal, he was *all over the place.* He taught the values of the heart."

He was probably also, although Philip will never say this, the first and clearest model for the teacher—both of the classroom and the heart—that Philip himself would be.

IT WAS A LIFE HE CAME to almost by accident, because of a teachers' strike, the worst in New York's history, that landed him in a fifth-grade classroom at P.S. 46 on 155th Street in Harlem, in the fall of 1968. It was the fall after the ghetto riots, the first since the murders of Kennedy and King—not a good time to be a white face in Harlem. But he needed a job, and a way out of the draft, and teaching was one route to a deferment. And from the first day, he says, he loved his time at the school.

"The kids were *incandescent with life*. There were

terrible racial tensions—Harlem was a hostile place in those days. But I made friends with some of my students' older brothers, we had kind of a social scene going. They looked at me, I think, as this kind of weird, wonderful hippie with long hair and glasses. So that made me all right, I guess, that helped me get by. I did get a black eye once, from being punched in the face when I went out to lunch in the neighborhood. But that only happened that one time."

He speaks often this way: back and forth between expansive, high-sounding declarations and the precise, understated syntax of the teacher he has been for much of the past forty years. His voice is soft, almost lulling sometimes—it is impossible to imagine him yelling—and he speaks with an earnestness accompanied often by small smiles. He is a very gentle man.

We met first on a February morning at his apartment on the Lower East Side of Manhattan, whose front door is flanked by two red decorative paper strips of Chinese characters. They are "spring couplets," Philip will tell me later, of "grammatically parallel verses," meant to welcome the visitor as he passes between them through the doors: "Take Up Brush and Paper" and "Fervently Love the Flowers of Spring." Philip, a devoted calligrapher, has brushstroked the verses himself.

The apartment itself is small but welcoming—like its owner—its living room washed in sunlight, the walls hung with a mix of Eastern art and French engravings. We will eat out today, at a cramped little luncheonette on

Third Avenue where Philip will begin the story of the last forty-five years of his life; other days he will cook our lunch himself, and serve it on a table by the window in the living room: chicken or seafood with salad, a bottle of white wine, and for dessert one day, a homemade flan with cream sauce.

I would have known him anywhere, and tell him so. Of the dozen or so classmates I've met to this point, he is the closest to my memory of him: short and slender, almost frail-seeming, and very fair, with long, delicate features and light brown hair that is now halfway to gray. In that 1958 third-form photo, he is in the third row, to the right of John Cocroft, looking straight out at the camera with the same quiet intensity, a serenity almost, I see in his face today.

His story, as he tells it, unfolds slowly over the weeks, and by degrees of privateness. Much of the first day, and also the second, we will talk about his family, his teaching, his calligraphy, his travels to West Africa and the Far East. Also his four years at Harvard, where he studied nineteenth-century English and French history and literature (his mother is French; he has spoken the language since childhood), was deeply involved in theater—he acted with John Lithgow, who remains a friend today—wrote his senior thesis on the politics of Charles de Gaulle, and graduated with honors in the spring of 1966. Harvard, he says, was "a place that let you find your own level. There was the party crowd, the revelers, who used to parade past my windows with their banners on football weekends in the fall. I wasn't one of those—but I enjoyed watching them, and I liked knowing they were there."

Two of his roommates at Harvard were former classmates from St. Paul's. One of these was Peter Johnson. When Philip talks about Peter, it is with a mix of pain and bafflement which, you get the sense, he has been carrying with him a long time.

"He was a brilliant person. A *passionate* person. He had so many gifts. There was this tremendous wit. And the sheer joy he took in language—he could be witty, malicious, erotic, his talents were almost limitless."

By the end of his second year at Harvard, Philip tells me, Peter's involvement as a writer for *The Lampoon* had pushed aside most everything else in his life. ("He was there every day, it was all he did, all he talked about, I don't know if he was even going to class.") His grades collapsed. He was told to take a year's absence. Six months later, in February 1965, he enlisted in the Army's Officer Candidates School, and after that at the School for Special Warfare at Fort Bragg, North Carolina, where he would finish twelfth in a class of 169. Sometime during this period, probably in the spring of 1966, he returned for a day-long visit to Harvard, where he and Philip and some others shared a lunch:

"He looked the same, except his hair was shorter. And he was wearing civilian clothes. But that was all that was the same. He made no mention at all of any of the things he'd loved before—*The Lampoon,* books, writing, nothing. It had all been replaced by this *total passion* for military life. It wasn't political, it wasn't about the war or anything like that—just this immersion he had now in the 'life of the soldier,' 'the military way.' He was *consumed* by it. It was all he talked about; he even tried to persuade us to join. I was dumbstruck. I think I must have backed away. There was no context anymore. I had nothing to say to him."

That was the last time they would see each other. When Philip learned of Peter's death—"instantly, by rifle fire" in the Vietnamese highlands nearly two years later—his first, "overcoming reaction" was to its needlessness.

"He was always a rebel. He fought things, he did things his own way. It was as if he needed something he could give himself to, something to be submerged in. And now, finally, he'd found it. Only it could have been *anything*. It could have been writing, a job, a person, a cause, anything. But it had to be *that*—the soldier thing. Something fatal, something that took his life. What an awful waste."

PHILIP'S FATHER, AUGUST HECKSCHER, was an intellectual in the old European sense of the term. And a towering one. Cultivated, broadly educated, descended from a family of eighteenth-century Hamburg bankers, he served, at one time or another, as an instructor of government at Yale, chief editorial writer for the *New York Herald Tribune,* director of the Twentieth Century Fund, commissioner of parks for the city of New York, and special consultant on the arts for the Kennedy White House. He was also on the board of half the museums, libraries, schools (including St. Paul's), and opera houses you could name, and wrote, depending on how you count them, something like twenty books—including at least two presidential biographies and a history of St. Paul's, from which he had graduated in 1932. He died in 1997. His wife, Claude, Philip's mother (with whom he still shares tea in the city at least weekly), is the daughter of a French high-court judge.

"So you see," Philip explains early in our first visit. ("*So you see*," always delivered with a little smile, sometimes, in our case, with a "*Geoffrey,*" is a common preamble with Philip.) "So you see, there was a strong tradition of public service. Strong but quiet. Almost as though it were something in the air."

In the fall of 1966, three months out of Harvard, Philip enrolled at Princeton's Woodrow Wilson School of Public and International Affairs. Founded in 1930 in honor of his father's favorite president, with a mission of "preparing talented individuals for careers in the service of the nation and the world"—"turning out technocrats for government," as Philip thinks of it today—it was a very high-octane sort of place.

He stayed two years—so miserable some days that he would retreat to the library with the *Herald Tribune* poetry column and "just weep." (Poetry, he explains, was "the only thing I could turn to, in that cold, cold place, with the power to move me to tears.") At the end of it all, he failed his economics requirement, suffered something like a breakdown, and—despite a formal petition by fellow students—left the school without a degree.

THERE ARE CERTAIN PEOPLE, you hear it said sometimes, who are "not meant for this world." If that can be said meaningfully of anyone, it could probably be said of Philip. But not in the sense of a failure to thrive—he seems clearly to be thriving—more in the sense, say, that thirty stranded travelers would see a broken-down bus while one might see a chance to share his bag of donuts.

It seems natural to him, even obvious, that poetry would be an antidote to economics. He keeps an email address on a decade-old system he rarely uses and seems almost to fear ("It's always breaking down."), but will write me a letter in elegant italics in thanks for the loan of a book. When I arrive one day at his apartment with a friend who is looking for directions to a bookstore, he will not hear of her leaving until she has stayed for lunch. He chokes up at odd moments, his eyes filmy, his throat grown suddenly thick.

The reason he loves to travel, he says, is the same reason he once thought, wrongly, he might want to work for the government—because it gives him the chance to "love widely in the world." When I ask why he wasn't more fearful during his teaching days in Harlem, he smiles gently and replies that "I was just too innocent, I suppose," then adds that even when he was mugged one day on the street, "I really didn't mind very much."

And nearly every day, often for many hours, in his East Village apartment, or for several weeks each summer in a cabin in Maine without plumbing or electricity, he will practice his calligraphy: arm extended, brush vertical to his body, in circular strokes on the rice paper—sometimes Daoist sayings or Zen poetry, other times satires on Maoist propaganda ("Defiantly Promote the Cultivation of Marijuana"). He has exhibited in several galleries, gives frequent private lessons, and has taught it in high schools as part of a state-funded program for the arts. But more than anything else, he says, he thinks of it as a spiritual expression, not unlike meditation, and with parallels to music or dance: "You have the score that someone else has written; your goal is to find yourself in it, to unite the meaning with your art." Then he adds, in the same soft voice, as if tone-deaf to the dissonance: "I practice like a son of a bitch."

HE IS GAY. HIS EARLIEST MEMORY of knowing this, he tells me—it is our third visit now, toward the end of May at a burger place near his home, the first time he has mentioned his gayness—was as a fourth- or fifth-grader at the Allen-Stevenson School in New York, an all-boys' school, where he'd been cast as Tessa in a production of *The Gondoliers*. "You look so lovely," a parent said to him after all the characters had been made up and dressed. "All the ninth-graders are in love with you, you know."

"I remember that moment vividly," he says. "I was terrified. I was sure I'd been found out."

I have no memory at St. Paul's of Philip being referred to as a "homo" (and there were several in the class who were) or of thinking of him that way myself. He was much of what he is today: serene, brainy, soft-spoken, quietly intense. He had a dignity, even then, and it was recognized. He was class secretary, president of the dramatic club (where he played Caesar, then Antony, to John Kerry's Metellus Cimber), editor of the school paper, a member of the sixth-form council. He studied calligraphy with the school's resident artist, wrote for the literary magazine, was a tenor in the choir. He would have been on anyone's list of the top five brains in the class.

But all the while he was struggling with his secret, and against his longings. When he was attracted to a boy, he tells me, he made a friend of him—but never showed his interest, never let it be known: "It was *something* at least. It was a way to get closer, a kind of sublimation, I suppose. And I really think they *knew*."

But if they knew, they never faced him with their knowing. Through four years at St. Paul's, then four more at Harvard: "I lived in fear. I guarded my secret. I had crushes right and left."

Recalling him as a classmate—the sense of peace he gave off, what seemed his easy poise—it's hard to imagine he was walking around with such pain. I tell him this, on the phone one day between my home in New Hampshire and his apartment in New York.

"I wouldn't call it pain, exactly. I was never conscious of hurting, only of being afraid. I was afraid of being *found out*. You have this *secret*—it isolates you, it alienates you, you can never relax, you can never trust, you can never be part of a group. Because then they might find out. And they would feel disdain for you, they could even *hate* you, and no one ever wants to be hated . . .

"And you can't be part of their group anyway—you don't want to be, not really—because their group carries their values. And their values are *anti-you*."

He remembers a moment, he says, when he was still young, still in his mid-twenties—but old enough to know who he was—when he looked out a bus window one day and saw a man he recognized as gay. And for that one moment at least, the group's values swallowed his.

"I looked at him—I don't remember what he looked like, I only remember looking—and I thought, 'He's gay,' or 'He's a fag,' or whatever it was I thought. And I was *revolted* by him. I actually felt revulsion. And then I thought—it was almost the same instant—*'How can this be? You're looking at yourself . . .'*

"So you see, that's the great danger of growing up gay in this country—the danger of loathing yourself."

Sometime toward the end of his time at Woodrow Wilson (he seems reluctant here to offer details, and I don't press for them), he met a ballet dancer in New York, named Michael, and fell in love. "Really in love," he tells me, "not just the physical thing. It was my first time."

There was a period of furtiveness. He doesn't say how long. When the rumors reached his parents, he decided the time had come.

"It was hard for them. My mother told me afterward that for her, for six months the sun didn't shine. But they loved me. And they saw that I was in love. And that love, in the end, was just love."

IT WAS DURING THIS SAME PERIOD, following his breakdown at Woodrow Wilson, that Philip went to work for the fifth-graders at P.S. 46. It was the start of an ascendant time for him. Coming off the shame of public failure and however many years of private fears, he unfolded himself now: a gay man, a teacher, the self-discovered product of his own searches and struggles, arriving on a stage that was finally, unshakably, his own. He enjoyed coupledom with his new lover; he found a joy in teaching children that would enrich him for much of the rest of his life.

"Michael and I were living together—at least at the beginning—in a five-floor walk-up on Ninety-third and Third, one of those old tenements with the bathtub in the kitchen and the toilet out in the hallway that everybody on the floor had to share—I think we paid about

$35 a month. There were a lot of music students in the next building—everybody knew everybody else in the neighborhood—and we used to lay a board across the air shaft between apartments and pass each other sugar and milk.

"In the summer we'd all go up on the roof and have 'tar beach parties'—you've *never* been to a tar beach party?—where we'd take our radios and blankets and sun cream and whatever, and just sit up there in our bathing suits in the sunshine surrounded by the chimneys and the TV antennas, and just talk and listen to music half the day . . .

"And on Sundays, at Bethesda Fountain in Central Park, where everybody, all the hippies, would be dressed up in their own ideas of fashion—beautiful outfits, outrageous outfits, whatever—and the whole idea was just to see and be seen . . .

"It was just a really good time. A *joyful* time. Very loving and very communal—I guess you'd say we were all hippies, and we were. But it was more than that. I found my generation those years."

I remember some of those same feelings. Philip was living on Ninety-third Street; I had moved down to the Village by then. He's gay and I'm straight and our scenes and situations were different—but it almost doesn't matter. I remember the crowds of tie-dyed T-shirts on Sheep Meadow in the summers, where you could almost sniff the air and get high, and the lines outside *Yellow Submarine* at the theater on Fourteenth Street, and sitting in the Riviera Café on Sheridan Square with Gabriella on Earth Day in 1970, watching the square fill with marchers with green-and-white banners who flowed in from the side streets like rivers converging. There was an energy in those moments ("It could be almost scary sometimes," Philip says), a sense of power and purpose, of belonging to something very large and righteous and unstoppable, that was enough to make you feel almost drunk.

HE STAYED TWO YEARS AT P.S. 46, until June of 1970, the same month I graduated from Stony Brook. His draft eligibility had ended by then, as had the relationship with Michael. The walk-up on Ninety-third Street was closing down for demolition; he was the last tenant left in the building. At Altamont Speedway in California, the December before, the last rock concert of the sixties had ended with the beating death of a teenager. Five months later, in May 1970, four war-protesting students would be shot dead by the National Guard at Kent State. For a lot of us that year, and maybe also for Philip, there was the feeling of something being over.

That same fall or winter, with a Woodrow Wilson classmate named Eric, a Dutchman who'd gotten a job with the Quaker Church, he traveled to tiny Togo, a poor, recently decolonized, phosphate-mining nation on the south coast of West Africa between Ghana and Benin. For the next year or so, working for the Quakers, he helped arrange conferences on education, self-government, and the role of women: "to break down and reshape, in any ways we could, the old colonial roles."

It was during that year in Togo, he says, that his sense of his worldly purpose first began to take real shape. He has a hard time explaining this, and his efforts to do so never quite sound the same way twice. But it comes down to the same sort of archetypal Christian ethic, so impossibly high-minded, that he talks about all the time: of "loving widely in the world."

"When you travel, when you go somewhere—it can be anywhere really, it can be a two-day round-trip—you have this wonderful opportunity to be intimate with people without investment, without any next chapter or last chapter, without any drag on it, without any present or past . . .

"*Think* about it. There you are, you're just passing through—you have nothing in common—you've come out of nowhere, you have nowhere to go. You can put yourself at service, you can be a conduit for ideas. You can love everybody, and they can love you."

It was just this way in Togo, he says: "I fell *in love* with the place. The same way you fall in love with a person—the same cherishing, the same hurt when you leave it or lose it. Because the *people* were all that mattered there. If a man got a flat tire while he was driving, all the cars behind him would stop, the people would get out and gather round, get up on their hoods and listen to music, keep the man company while he changed the tire on his car. It was beautiful to be a part of that . . .

"I've been back there since then. It's changed, it's not the same anymore. And it hurt *so much* to see that. I can't go back again, I don't think. Maybe not ever. I love the memory too much."

Later the same afternoon he tells me all this—it is our second meeting—on our way back together from the burger place near his home, we pass a sidewalk book dealer, a young Indian man with a stack of used volumes on a rickety table near the curb. Philip stops, smiles—it is as if they are resuming a conversation. (". . . So, my friend, will you be here tomorrow? I will have some books for you . . .") It's the same way an hour later, sharing a taxi uptown with him, with a silent, pock-faced, eastern-European driver at the wheel. By the time I get off at my stop (Philip is going on to meet his mother uptown), the cabbie is swiveled halfway around in his seat, laughing, exclaiming, going on about the cost of living in Bucharest or Kiev.

HE RETURNED FROM TOGO, WITH ERIC, in the summer of 1971, found a job as recreation director at the boat basin at Manhattan's Riverside Park. For that year and most of the next, he planned events, refereed softball games, rented rowboats, and spent a lot of time—especially in winter—in a small office in the playground by himself. ("A park is a lonely place in winter. You see some strange things. I remember there was this one family, the wife and children of a minister of some odd, monkish sect, very strange people, who used to come and play by themselves on a seesaw in the snow. And there were rumors—I never saw it happen, but I wouldn't be surprised—of babies, black-market babies, being exchanged in the parking garage underneath where I was.")

What was he thinking? He was twenty-seven by now, gifted, Harvard-educated, with a family legacy that could have opened almost any door—making his living tending a city park. And it's not as if this was some hippie-phase anomaly. As life patterns go, it was only just getting under way. So what did he think about those long winter days in his little office in the park? Did he wonder about where life was taking him? Did he ever worry that he might not be living up to his gifts—or to his father's hopes?

He probably worried. And certainly he felt his father's weight. ("My father's whole life," he says, "was a forum for achievement. It's hard not to be affected by that.") You couldn't spend eight years at St. Paul's and Harvard—much less as August Heckscher's son—and not feel that there were expectations involved.

And for the longest time, he had delivered. He had excelled. Honors scholar, singer, actor, editor, class officer, everything but an athlete—at St. Paul's, they'd had to tell him to stop taking on new posts. Then Woodrow Wilson. A diplomat's career-in-waiting. Everything his father could have hoped.

And then he crashed. Just broke down, like an overtrained thoroughbred. And never raced the same race again.

There's no way of knowing why it happened as it did—why then and not later, why such a terminal blow. But it's a story we've all heard before: so much pressure for so long to do so well, until one day, one load too many, you just crack. The pressure in Philip's case was mostly self-applied (his father, from everything he tells me, was not the bullying sort), but that can sometimes be the worst kind. It's also possible there was something like instinct involved: a temperament such as Philip's—gentle, spiritual, poetic, not given to confrontation—may have lacked the hard edges needed for a diplomatic career. He may have sensed this (or discerned it somehow in the economics course that brought on his collapse) and simply shut himself down. However it happened, I can't imagine it wasn't for the best. He's as far from an Albright or a Kissinger as anyone I know.

But why such total abdication? Why from Woodrow Wilson to Harlem to Togo to the shed at Riverside Park? Was this some sort of defiance? Or was there an epiphany involved? The answer to this comes straight from Philip—though he never meant it in answer to anything I asked:

"The sixties were an emancipation for me. The sense of alienation I carried, as a gay man, of being always outside of the group—it fit right in with that whole anti-establishment thing. *Everyone* was alienated, the *whole generation* was alienated, that's what it was all about. So I felt empowered by that—I don't like that word, but it fits. A lot of people were empowered by the sixties, I think: to be gay, to be artists, to seek alternatives. To not be yoked by expectations, to just let yourself fully be."

HE AND ERIC RENTED A LOFT over a wholesale florist shop near Herald Square, a sprawling, sunny place, the just-vacated home of the Bright Star Embroidery Company, where they would live together, though never as more than close friends ("We were opposite types—Eric was a big drinker, a hard liver, very passionate and direct."), for almost five years. Their neighbors were an artist couple who made their living writing porn, and another couple who turned their loft, on Wednesday nights, into an unlicensed restaurant they called The Silky Valentine. On clear nights sometimes, they would go up on the roof, get high, and watch the lights go out at midnight on the Empire State Building next door. "It was like this giant switch being flipped," Philip says.

A year or so after they moved there, he went one day with a friend, a black Tennesseean named Howard, to a gospel church in Harlem that Howard had been talking about. It was the First Tabernacle of Deliverance Spiritual Church, housed in a storefront on 125th Street and Lenox Avenue which, until not long before, had been a beauty parlor owned and run by Jackie Robinson's wife. It was a modest place: long and narrow—a typical New York storefront—lit by a street-side plate-glass window, with a center aisle bisecting rows of folding chairs leading to a candlelit altar draped in cloth. There were no more than seventy-five members, he guesses, and not another white face to be seen. But for Philip, as he would write years later in a brief, elegiac memoir of his time there: "I had never felt so much a part of a community before."

It happened from the first Sunday. The gospel choir ("whose sound seemed huge, three-dimensional and all-pervasive in that low, rectangular space"), the passion of the young pastor's sermon, followed by the responses from his flock: "Tell it, Rev! Go on, now, it's the truth!" Then came the heart of the service: the choir and congregation on their feet, spontaneously, in ones and twos, whooping and hugging themselves ("getting the spirit"), hugging each other, calling on Jesus, then commencing a rapid, jerky, weight-shifting two-step—forward-back, forward-back, first joined, then led, by the organ—that had them, within not many seconds, stomping their feet, clapping their hands, tipping over then tossing aside chairs to make space for the dance that will follow—which could only be described as ecstatic.

"I find tears pouring down my face," writes Philip in remembrance. "I'm trembling, emotionally spent and strangely elated. *This* to me is what the early church must have been, when the Holy Ghost was real and worship was spontaneous—so far from the decorous, formalized Episcopalian services of my childhood and St. Paul's."

He went the next Sunday, and the next. And every Sunday, at the same point in the service, the pastor would make the same appeal: "Now I know there are those out there who are thinking of becoming brothers and sisters with us. Well, all you have to do is *walk*—just walk down this aisle, and you'll be one with us." And on the third or fourth Sunday, with the organ swelling and the pastor at the altar with his arms spread wide, Philip walked.

And that was the start of it. For the three or four years that followed, he sang as a tenor in the First Tabernacle choir: a long-haired, bespectacled white boy singing, "Leaning on the Everlasting Arm" and "There Is No Hiding Place" alongside the stout older ladies and the older and younger black men. Wherever the choir went, he went with it: to rehearsals every Thursday, "fellowship concerts" at churches as far away as Dayton, even once to Los Angeles to sing for the bishop in Tabernacle's anchor church there. He was mugged once—turned upside down, his pockets emptied, watched silently by a block-long line of stoop-sitters on 128th Street on a humid summer night—badly scared another time and jeered at or taunted too many times to care. "I was oblivious," he says today. "Just caught up in things, I guess."

As a small boy, like most of us, he had been baptized in the Episcopal Church. It would have been a formal affair, administered by a black-clad clergyman from a Gothic font under stained-glass windows, with his parents, godparents, and relatives, in suits and gay-colored dresses, seated across most of the first several pews. It had happened, in his case, in Auburn, New York, where he had lived until he was three or four.

It happened for the second time in Los Angeles in 1973—he was twenty-nine—in front of the municipal changing rooms at Venice Beach at seven in the morning. All involved were dressed in white robes, clapping and singing in unison, "Take Me to the Water to Be Baptized." The bishop and his assistant were some ways from shore, waist-deep in the water, when Philip waded out to them, his robe drenched, his Beatles haircut blowing in the sea breeze, to be gripped by the chest and back and plunged, backward, into the sea.

The memoir he wrote, in which this account is mostly contained, is twenty-eight pages long, handwritten, double-spaced on lined paper. It is a gentle and elegant record, very much an act of love. It came to me in the mail one early spring day, at my request, nearly a year after our first meeting in New York. I called him one morning soon after. We talked for a while about his time at First Tabernacle, and about what became of it—the storefront church, he said, is long since gone. Then I asked his thoughts on God. He seemed surprised by the question, and didn't answer right away. When he did, it was with a story that was so familiar I had to interrupt him halfway through to tell him it had happened, the same way exactly, to me:

"On Sunday nights [at St. Paul's] at the evensong service, listening to the organ and to all those sonorous, uplifting verses and prayers, I would sometimes be very moved. It could feel so comforting, you know? So, sort of, *majestic*—you could almost feel a sense of something divine, whatever that may have meant at sixteen. So I'd sit there in my pew and I'd ask God, 'Please, if you're out there, send me a sign of some sort, a blue light or something, so I'll know.'"

I laugh into the phone and tell him I used to do the same thing exactly, also at the evensong service, and sometimes, too, at the organ recital that followed—and I never got an answer, either. He continues talking as if I hadn't said a thing: "Then I went to Tabernacle, and I knew *right away.* There was never any doubt. There was a spirit. I wept. My emotions had been touched."

It's hard to know what he means by this exactly—God, spirit, and emotion are elusive values, hard to connect or separate in any way that will mean the same thing to two people. But I've thought about his words a lot, and I'd like to think I know. There he was, an upper-class, overeducated gay white man, still lonely in his gayness, probably still fighting self-hate, being welcomed unconditionally—as a soul and as a singer—by a congregation of poor and middle-class blacks in the heart of 1970s Harlem. No wonder he wept. No wonder he saw God in the weeping. There was *forgiveness* in that storefront: for being gay, for being white, for hating yourself, for anything you needed. There was forgiveness and acceptance—*Christian love*—of the kind they only preached at St. Paul's.

And for Philip, whose life up to then, like most of ours, had been a search for belonging, there must have been a very great peace:

"School and experience had taught me to think for myself," he writes toward the end of his memoir, "while the sixties exalted autonomy. Tabernacle folks seemed part of an older, more traditional model, where the group took precedence . . . a leveling mechanism that assured that those who sank too low would be cared for, those who rose above would be chastened. What counted was the *middle,* where the community was cushioned from change."

LATE ONE FALL TOWARD THE END of his time with the church, the call went out for a venue large enough to host a First Tabernacle Thanksgiving Day dinner: pastors, musicians, choir, congregation, and anyone they'd bring. There was only one real option, as it turned out, nearly 130 blocks downtown. It was Philip and Eric's loft:

"The kitchen, with its modest four-burner stove and counters made of hollow doors, was taken over by women skilled at feeding a hungry crowd. They brought a turkey and ham, rice and greens, macaroni and cheese, cakes and pies from their own ovens in large foil pans turbanned in more foil. Disco and rock music blared from my inadequate amplifiers, and the big windows in front, seen from the street, were filled with swirling, dancing figures. Animated card games took place on the tables, the bed, the floor. The elders were given the few available chairs, where they sat nodding, smiling, observing the animation around them as they might from front porches in rural, Southern places. The loft was filled as never before, filled to its skylights with smoke and laughter and music and talk. It seemed as if the soul of Harlem, a soul of celebration and human warmth, had come downtown for the evening."

Outside the Circle

"Hey, you walking back with anybody?" I say that no, I'm not—even though I know that he knows this already—and he falls in beside me, talking a mile a minute, his helmet in his hand.

"That was a nice run, at the end there, when you faked out Whitman like that," he says to me—or something just like that, some small kiss-up to get things going, even though he must know that I already know what he wants. (I hardly know him; I hardly know anyone, none of us do, we've only

been at the school two weeks—but in this case you'd have to be an idiot not to know what he wants with me.)

"You're really fast. A lot faster than me. I'd say you're the fastest on the team."

I tell him thanks, and agree that I probably am. It's nice to hear him say it, though. He's a good player. Quick with his feet, and really dodgy, and he can put a better spiral on the ball, and maybe throw it harder, than anybody else on the team. The coach will probably make him quarterback—which was the position I wanted to play originally, but I can't pass the way he can, so I'll probably just play halfback or end.

"Made up your mind how you're going to vote tomorrow? Who you want as captain?"

No, I say, I haven't decided yet. Which is true. (I wish he hadn't come up to me. He makes me nervous. He talks really fast, including with his hands when he's excited, and he gets right up close to your face, and he won't let anything go. It just makes you want to run away.)

"Well, look, you can vote for Riley if you want to—it's absolutely up to you." He is talking faster now; we're halfway back to the lockers. "I like *Riley, I do, he's a good guy. But he's a lineman, he's a tackle. And I'm in the backfield, like you. Have you thought about the difference that could make?"*

I say that no, actually, I haven't thought about it at all.

So he explains. It is a long explanation, and very complicated; we are back at the lockers long before it is done. And there we stand, the two of us, still all sweaty in our pads and jerseys, the other kids running back and forth around us to the showers in their towels, while John re-creates plays from that day's scrimmage, and from games and scrimmages that haven't happened yet—all by way of proving to me what I never would have come to on my own: that having another backfielder (as opposed to a lineman) as team captain—and therefore in a position to look out for my interests, and to represent them to the coach—is an advantage I wouldn't want to turn my back on, and am fortunately in a position to ensure—through a vote for him the next day.

I am dazzled. No one in my life (I am thirteen, the same age as John) has ever before petitioned me for anything, much less with such understanding, such careful concern for what might be best for me. I know, of course, that he might not mean it—might not mean a word of it—that his only real interest is my vote. But it doesn't matter. I am too thrilled and flattered not to promise it, then to raise my hand for him the next day.

And fourteen years later, when I will see him again for the first time in ten years, on the little black-and-white TV in my girlfriend's apartment outside Boston, sitting in his green, medal-pinned navy fatigues with his hands folded in front of him, asking: "How do you ask a man to be the last man to die for a mistake?"—the first thought I will have will be of that afternoon on the path back to the lockers, and of the gift that he'd had, even then.

EVERYTHING HAD BEGUN WITH JOHN. The emails, the slow reuniting, the shame unloosed by Arthur, my search for the heart of the class—it had all begun with him. And he was the first I had called and written, when he was newly his party's nominee for president, in the summer of 2004.

He was the last I would meet: almost exactly a year later, eight months after he had lost the election, in his office in the Russell Building in Washington, with his press secretary taking notes on a couch in the corner, in July of 2005. The appointment was scheduled for forty-five minutes. It lasted exactly that.

I had met by then with all the others I'd be meeting, in most cases more than once; and there were meetings still to come. We had shared meals; I had been in some of their homes, met some of their wives, read their stories on email, looked at their family photos, listened to their memories, and shared a lot of my own. I had come to know them, at least in this narrow sense. And in two or three of the cases, by the time the process had unwound itself, there was something close to friendship there.

There was none of this with John. He sat behind a big desk in a big office; I sat across from him, with the press secretary between us, and I asked questions and he responded until our time was done. Then I left. I never talked to him or heard from him again.

There are a lot of things I wish I'd done differently that day. I wish, for one, that I'd thought to tell him what it had meant to me to see him, that evening so many years before, on Gabriella's little TV. I was twenty-seven by then—it was 1971—living in Boston and writing for underground papers. The colleges, the nothing jobs, and most of the messiness were behind me. But I was still not done with the gambling troubles—spending most of my afternoons at the track—and was drinking now even more than before. I was still badly adrift. But if you'd asked me, I'd probably have told you I was learning about writing and life.

Seeing John on the news that April night, once I'd gotten past the first shock, left me with a flatness I couldn't shake for days. I hadn't thought of him in years; I don't remember if I'd even known he was in Vietnam. And now here he was in a hearing room of the Senate, being applauded by men who were heroes to me—William Fulbright, Jacob Javits—saying the same things I said and heard every night in someone's bar or living room. But he had won Purple Hearts, led fearful men down strange Asian rivers, and come home to tell what he had seen. I listened to "Masters of War" stoned on headphones and quoted Pete Hamill's columns to friends.

By the time he had finished—with a vow to "search out and destroy the last vestige of this barbaric war, to pacify our own hearts, to conquer the hate and fear that has divided this country these last ten years and more"—I felt the smallness of my days as I had rarely felt it before.

If there had been more time that day, or other things had been easier, I might have told him all this. And it might just have reached him, it might have bridged the gulf—and our time then might have been different. But I didn't. And in the end, it was what it was: a senator not known for his looseness being solicited by an old classmate he only vaguely remembered who wanted to talk about old times. It was a bad script to begin with. Probably neither of us was expecting very much.

THERE WAS A LOT SAID AND written during the 2004 campaign about the "enigma" John Kerry presented: the Swift Boat toughness, the Brahmin aloofness, the odd, sometimes crippling judgment lapses, the loner mentality in a man so needing to be liked. The essence of a lot of it was similar: that John was an independent spirit, driven but complex; that he had a soft side but was hard to reach; that he could be ruthlessly focused; that he didn't make friends easily but was fiercely loyal when he did.

What I came away with, mostly, was how in line all this sounded with the schoolboy I remembered: how little it seemed he had changed. A cover article in *Newsweek* called him "the solitary soldier"—John at St. Paul's was as solitary as I was, as solitary as anyone I knew. But not because he was a Catholic among Protestants, or a liberal among the sons of 1950s Republicans, or because his family lacked outright wealth—all of which the press adopted as dogma. I never knew or heard mentioned, in the four years we were classmates, that he wasn't as Episcopal as the rest of us, or as rich. And no one, anyway, would have cared. Money was flaunted, but rarely talked about; and religion, like politics, was mostly just assumed.

No. The reason John was solitary (and probably lonely, as he has said at times that he was) was that he was more *serious* than the rest of us. More serious even than the serious ones, which would probably have included me. He was intense, distant, aloof, mostly humorless. He cared too much about things: soccer, hockey, the drama club, the debate club, the larger world. He tried too hard. He rarely smiled, he rarely joked. He wasn't cool.

"I can remember him sitting on my sofa in the evenings, talking a long, long time," Herb Church, a lifelong St. Paul's English teacher, and the faculty head of John's senior-year dorm, told a reporter four years ago, not long before he died. "I thought this was a man who might go somewhere . . . The thing that impressed me was his very serious idealism. A lot of guys wanted to be head of Daddy's Wall Street firm—nothing wrong with that. But this young guy, you had the feeling he would do something for the world. He was a sincere idealist."

"I marched to my own drummer," John has said—and would say to me when we finally got together—more than once. And it was true. He did. Which was why he always seemed, to the rest of us, so inscrutable. And why his friends were so few. It is why, even today—depending on who's telling the story—there may be boos from classmates at the mention of his name.

The only real friend he had at St. Paul's (though I never knew at the time that they were friends) was a boy named Dan Barbiero, another high-achiever, whose Italian surname and middle-class origins kept him as far from the mainstream as John. I had lunch with Dan in New York not long after the election, and he talked with me about both John and the school:

"I was just an Italian kid who went to choir school since sixth grade. And the first week I'm at St. Paul's, I meet these two guys, two separate guys—Heckscher and Floyd—and both of them tell me, at different times, that there's a highway named after their family on Long Island. And I'm thinking, 'This can't be, this just can't be—two guys, both in my form, both with highways named after them. Wow, this is sure some kind of school.'"

Dan and John were roommates their last two years at St. Paul's, and would be again, through all four years at Yale. It is a closeness that continues today:

"John has trouble making friends. He always did. That's just how he is—he can seem cold and aloof to some people, but he's not really, he just doesn't know how to seem any other way. He's really warm once you take the time to know him. And loyal, very loyal."

He was *stiff,* is I think what Dan was trying to say. Stiff, out of step, and mostly friendless—which, at fifteen or sixteen, in that seething, hermetic little culture, was enough to bring almost any of us to our knees.

But it didn't with John. And that was the remarkable thing. He never retreated, as I and others did: went inward, avoided contact, lived for vacations. And he didn't take John Cocroft's route and "borrow" anyone's brains or style. He *attacked*. Played every sport—all, by the end, at the varsity level—joined every club, literary board, and student society in sight (he even invented one). As his mentor, he chose the Reverend John Walker, the only black teacher at the school—who counseled him to reread Emerson's "Self-Reliance" whenever self-doubt raised its head. And on Election Day in 1960, quixotically or defiantly—with Lloyd, not yet our president, the advocate for the other side—he argued the case for John F. Kennedy, a hero to almost no one but him, in a debate before the top two forms in the school.

"He was a very focused person, in a culture where people were generally indirect about things," Philip Heckscher told a reporter the spring before the election. "And that might have made him seem ruthless to some."

He *did* seem ruthless, and calculating, and transparently ambitious—and *nothing* transparent was a virtue at St. Paul's. But it worked. He excelled. ("He was right and we were wrong," another classmate wrote in an email before the election. "Just look at what he's done.") And the more achievements he amassed, the more single-minded he became. And the thicker grew the wall between public and private, between the achiever and the boy.

IT'S NOT HARD TO TRACE THE roots of some of this: the remoteness, the self-reliance, the high-minded public-service ideals. John's father, Richard Kerry, was a distant, demanding man, embittered by his own father's early suicide and a sister's premature death. A career civil servant with postings in Washington, Oslo, and Berlin, he was a wartime test pilot, an ocean sailor, a risk-taker—a man's man—with visionary ideals about America and the world but neither the time nor the emotional makeup for children. ("I was always moving on and saying good-bye," John has said about his years at boarding school, which began—in Switzerland—at age ten. "It kind of had an effect on you, it steeled you. There wasn't a lot of permanence and roots.") At the dinner table—when there were family dinners at all—the talk was of politics and foreign policy. For John, a ten-year-old in postwar West Berlin, there must have been a strong sense of America as missionary to the world.

His mother, Rosemary Forbes, born and raised in France, the daughter of an émigré American shipping magnate, descended from the first governor of Massachusetts, had studied to be a nurse. She met her husband in the summer of 1938, in Saint-Briac-Sur-Mer on the coast of Brittany, the village of her father's estate, where Richard, then twenty-three, had come to study sculpting. Two years later, she would flee the village on a bicycle, hours ahead of the Nazis, leaving behind everything but his photo. ("Dick Dearest: It is a shock to find a country one has admired and loved crumbling away, eaten through to its very core by rottenness . . . We left Thursday, June 13 at 8:30 P.M., just after the gas and electricity had been shut off and explosions were going off where they were blowing up gasoline tanks . . . At dawn the Germans entered Paris.")

They were married in Alabama in January 1941. Six years later, the war over, they returned for a visit to Saint Briac—to find nothing left of the Forbes estate but a chimney and some stairs. For John, who was four years old, it would form the skeleton of a memory: "I remember the staircase in the sky, the glass under my feet, and [that] my mom was crying,"

So there is idealism on both sides. ("Integrity, integrity" were the last words his mother spoke to him, he says, before her death six years ago.) And self-reliance. And a strong internationalist streak. It's not hard to see how such a boy might grow up driven or reclusive, or might have trouble making friends.

BUT THE AMBITION IS SOMETHING ELSE. And it is the *ambition*—more, I think, than any other quality—that defines him, that has informed his decisions, guided his heroics, brought on his lowest moments, and accounted for the inscrutability, the sometimes-almost-schizophrenia, that may be the biggest reason he is not president today.

It was there when he asked for my vote, on our way back to the lockers on that fall day in 1957—though I don't know what he, or anyone, might have called it then. But by four or five years later, by the time he left St. Paul's for Yale in the fall of 1962, if you'd passed out a questionnaire to every member of the class—"Which classmate among us do you think most wants to be president?"—John Kerry would have been the ten-to-one choice.

"I wanted to be president of the United States when I was seventeen," Lloyd MacDonald told a reporter during the campaign, and later admitted to me over dinner. "And it was the last thing in the world you would admit to."

I wouldn't have guessed this about Lloyd, though I probably should have: he was class president, he had a good word for just about everyone, and most things he did and said (now that I think about it) cast a pretty wide net across the class. But he was *easy.* He laughed and talked like he meant it, he didn't showboat, he didn't chase the limelight; you never got the sense with Lloyd that he was forever sniffing the wind.

John wore his ambition the way the Regs wore their pinstripes. He pressed, he flaunted, he angled for the lights. On the hockey rink, he was "Keep-the-Puck Kerry," known more for his wide, swooping rink turns than for the goals he scored. ("He was one of the best stickhandlers on the team and welcomed the opportunity to exhibit his skills," John Cocroft remembered during the campaign. "Impatient cries of 'shoot' or 'pass it' would follow him whenever he got the puck, at which point he would execute one more rink-turn and turn a heads-up dribble, looking for a better opportunity.") His idolatry of John Kennedy was naked and shameless—he signed notes and papers with his "JFK" initials, there were reports that he Magic Markered them into the fabric of his jeans. In a school where you won or lost points by the languor you affected, these weren't qualities that were going to win him many friends.

"I think hatred is too strong a word," another classmate has said. "Loathing is too strong a word. He may have seemed a little calculating to some people, and perhaps to me as well at the time. But he wanted to be liked."

I HAD VOTED FOR HIM NINE months before, and began by telling him so. He thanked me for this, also for the modest contribution I'd made to his campaign, which he had apparently researched in advance: "We appreciate that, it means a lot." His smile was gracious, and seemed real. His press secretary, taking notes on a couch against the wall, also smiled.

Then I told the football story. I had planned this in advance: to break down the stiffness, remind him of the little bit of history we shared. I made a joke of it, said something about how I might have been the swing vote in his first-ever run for elective office, back when we were both thirteen (though I don't remember if he actually won that election or not). I was hoping to get a laugh out of this, maybe set a tone. Whatever it took to get him to see me as a classmate, not a writer—which I knew, long before I got there, was going to be the challenge of the day.

His face was a blank. No recognition, no humor, no

interest. It was as though I were speaking in a different language, or had just told some off-color story and he was trying his best to manage his disgust. "*Oh,*" he said. "There was an election? For team captain? I don't remember anything about that at all." He seemed off-balance—unprepared for such silliness—and both his face and his voice showed disdain.

We moved on, but the stiffness lingered. I asked him about his circle of friends at St. Paul's. "I had a small, intimate group of friends," he said. He named three. One was a boy I hadn't known in the class ahead of us; another was Peter Johnson, killed in Vietnam. I asked if he'd been happy at the school. He said that in general he had, and mentioned sports, a visit to the school by Robert Frost, the beauty of New Hampshire winters, and several other, smaller things. He said again what I'd read already, more than once, that the value of public service was first instilled in him at St. Paul's: "I just didn't know yet what shape it would take—journalism or politics, or something more like my dad."

He did admit to me, when I pressed him, that there had been times when he'd "felt a little awkward" at the school, that he'd resented the conformity and the "monastic" way of life. "Kids can be tough on each other," he said. "And I didn't really get the culture or the language they spoke." At some point I mentioned Arthur, who was still alive at the time and emailing us all on a near-daily basis. John shook his head slowly, made a clicking noise with his mouth, and said, "Yeah, a sad, sad guy."

We spent more time than I would have liked talking about Vietnam: his volunteering and early zealotry ("LBJ had asked us . . ." "I wanted to win . . ."); the choice of Swift Boats over a cruiser or destroyer ("I'm a small boat kind of guy . . ."); the gradual eroding of faith; the final turning point—the Tet Offensive—the trip back on the frigate when the news came of Bobby Kennedy's murder ("That's when I began to ask a lot of questions . . ."). I'd heard or read nearly all of this already, much of it in the same words he was using now. And he must have known this. He couldn't possibly have thought he was telling me anything new.

But it didn't seem to matter. It was almost as if, in the absence of any real agenda—Iraq, say, or nuclear testing or the economy—he was reverting to his default mode, his place of origins, the single, certain defining currency he had. Which seemed a pity to me. And still does.

There's not much else to say about those forty-five minutes. They passed slowly. John remained stiff, and seemed vaguely uncomfortable—I may have seemed the same to him—as though he was having trouble understanding why exactly I was there. From time to time he'd throw in some small piece of schoolboy vernacular (the old school store was "pretty cool," the surprise black-ice holidays were "a blast") as though he were trying to tell me he could still wear that old classmate hat. But even with that, the connection I'd hoped for never happened. It never came close.

There is something else I wish I'd said—I wouldn't think of it until later on the plane ride home, and might not have had the courage if I had. I wish I'd said that I'd always *known* he felt awkward. That I had as well. That both of us, in different ways, for different reasons, had been unhappy outsiders at St. Paul's.

But it wasn't the time or place for that kind of unburdening. And I expect he knew that anyway.

BY THE TIME OF HIS SOPHOMORE year at Yale in the fall of 1963, it would have been hard to mistake his focus. He'd been dating a Kennedy—Janet Auchincloss, half-sister to the president's wife, who would later marry his sixth-form roommate from St. Paul's—and was rooming now with Harvey Bundy, nephew of the Bundy brothers, William and McGeorge, both advisors in the JFK White House. He was about to be named president of the Yale Political Union, which would give him private audiences with governors, civil-rights leaders, and a half dozen members of the House. His liaison with Janet had earned him, even before his Yale career began, an invitation to Hammersmith Farm in Rhode Island—the scene, nine years earlier, of the Kennedy-Bouvier wedding—where he had met the president in the late summer of 1962. ("Hi, Mr. Kennedy," he remembers responding. "I just graduated from St. Paul's, I'm about to go to Yale.")

Somewhere between St. Paul's and the end of his freshman year at Yale, he must have learned not to try quite so hard—or at least not to wear it on his sleeve. He had real friendships at Yale: lasting ones, moneyed ones, connected ones, the kind of friendships the Ivy League is famous for. Probably the closest of these was with David Thorne, a nephew of Henry L. Stimson, a former secretary of state, and twin brother to Julia Thorne, whom John would meet his sophomore year and marry six years later. Another, older friend—they'd known each other since they were both about thirteen—was Dick Pershing, grandson of General "Black Jack" Pershing of San Juan Hill and World War I and son of Wall Street's Warren Pershing, my own father's boss and employer the last twenty-five years of his life. All three friends, upon their Yale graduation, would go to Vietnam. All but Pershing would return.

YALE WAS VERY GOOD TO JOHN, in most of the ways that college can be good. He played soccer and hockey, sharpened his debating skills, studied history, learned to laugh and to fly small planes, made contacts that would be useful and friends he would hold on to for life. These were the years he found his balance: his private dreams became public, his furtive manipulations became a visible, unfolding life plan.

"John would clearly say, 'If I could make my dream come true, it would be running for president of the United States,'" a Yale debate-team partner, William Stanberry, would say later. "It was not a casual interest. It was a serious, stated interest. His lifetime ambition was to be in political office. I don't think he had pet issues as much as he simply said, 'The life of the politician is the life I want. I want to speak out on issues. That's what I want to do.'"

The news of John Kennedy's assassination came to him during a soccer game midway through the first semester of his sophomore year at Yale. He spent the rest of that weekend and much of the next week—as a lot of us did, wherever we were, but it had to have been more personal for him—watching the reprisal and funeral, and Lee Harvey Oswald's killing, on the black-and-white TV in his room. Sometime later that year or early the year after, Yale would be visited by William Bundy, Kennedy's old advisor and now assistant secretary of state, who would come to speak in support of what by then was Lyndon Johnson's war. His speech ended, he would visit with his nephew Harvey, and Harvey's roommates, in their suite at Yale's Jonathan Edwards College.

"We were all drinking beer and sitting around and talking about, you know, Southeast Asia and domino [theories] and war," John would recall years later. Bundy's theme, as he remembered it, had been pretty straightforward that day: "We need you. We need you to go into the officer program and to go to Vietnam."

He would heed the call, but not without some very public doubts. In February 1966 he made his commitment to enlist in the navy's Officer Candidate School; five months later, on June 12, as senior-class orator at the Yale graduation, he delivered a speech that seems, in hindsight, both angry and ambivalent—and an oddly well-tuned foreshadowing of speeches to come:

"This Vietnam War has found our policy-makers forcing Americans into a strange corner . . . that if victory escapes us, it will not be the fault of those who lead but of the doubters who stabbed them in the back . . .

"We have not really lost the desire to serve. We question the very roots of what we are serving."

I haven't been able to find, either in the pages and pages I've read on John and his relationship to Vietnam or in the responses he would finally give me in person, a persuasive answer to the question: Why would he volunteer to serve in a war he seemed to already oppose? I assume the answer lies somewhere in the mix of his youth, his father's legacy, his Kennedy loyalties, and his own fast-blooming ambitions. One thing seems clear, though. He didn't have to do it. There were other options: family connections, graduate school, a teaching deferment, even the draft, which would probably have left him sitting in an office somewhere. He didn't have to fight.

But he chose to. A lot like at St. Paul's, when he was friendless and could have retreated but instead invented new clubs to join; or later in Vietnam, when he would—famously—run the boat he commanded directly *toward* the bullets from the beach. His approach, in hard times, is often the frontal assault. Boldness, ingenuity, the turning of tables. But not haphazardly, and not without knowing the risks.

"I do not want to rock-climb, I do not jump out of

airplanes," he would say years later, in disputing the charge of being a daredevil pilot—but he could just as easily have been talking about his approach to war or politics, or to life. "I [do] things where I think there's a technique that if you're disciplined you can master and be in control."

HE GRADUATED FROM YALE IN JUNE. The next eighteen months were spent in training, first at Navy OCS in Rhode Island, then for a year in California. By the time they shipped him out, to the Gulf of Tonkin in December 1967, it had become a very different war: close to 500,000 troops on the ground now, with 16,000 dead. The campuses were in spiraling protest; at the Pentagon, Robert McNamara had just resigned. A month later would come the Tet Offensive, and the news that Dick Pershing—then Peter Johnson—had been lost. ("Then I just cried—a pathetic and very empty kind of crying that turned into anger and bitterness.")

It's hard not to believe, reading his letters, that this was a time of real pain. He was just twenty-four. Everything up to now had been all dreams and talk, possibilities and high intentions—St. Paul's, Yale, navy officer, athlete, flier, class orator, kid pretender to the Kennedy name. Everything rich and golden and blessedly manifest: life, even greatness, just a turn or two ahead down the road—the kidders at Yale, when he walked into a room, playing "Hail to the Chief" on the kazoo.

And now his oldest friend dead, killed instantly, of a grenade attack in a rice paddy in a hamlet called Hung Nhon in a war that, in the dorm rooms and classrooms of New Haven, had been talk-fodder for boys and young men. And he had been the handsome one, the charmer, the joker, the drinker, the reprobate; the one who, it was said, always knew every girl in the bar. Gone now. Just like that. ("Time will never heal this," John wrote to his parents that month.)

It was Julia Thorne, whom he would marry two years later, who had sent him the telegram with the news that Dick Pershing was dead. He wrote her back: a less mournful letter than the one to his parents, more anguished, more filled with the anger and sense of perversity that would seem to consume him by the time he was done with Vietnam. And again now, there was purpose—an early version of that same refrain about mastery and self-control.

> I have never in my life been so alone with something like this before. I feel so bitter and angry and everywhere around me there is nothing but violence and war and gross insensitivity. I am really very frightened to be honest . . .
>
> Right now everything that is superficial and emotional wants to give up and just feel sorry but I can't. There is a beast in me that keeps pushing me on saying Johnny you can't let go because of this—Johnny

> you find some sense from this—Johnny you are too strong to stop now—something keeps me going harder than before. Judy, if I do nothing else in my life I will never stop trying to bring to people the conviction of how wasteful and asinine is a human expenditure of this kind . . .
>
> Two aircraft carriers are now in port . . . the talk is of pilots lost and [air] strikes that were successful for the number of lives taken or unsuccessful for the number of lives lost—both the same and both creating the same hole and sorrow for some unsuspecting person somewhere . . . Anyone could at some time for the same stupid irrational something that stole Persh be gone tomorrow.

Three months later King would be dead, then Bobby Kennedy; and Lyndon Johnson would give himself up. The U.S. dead passed twenty-five thousand. Eugene McCarthy filled baseball stadiums with his earnest, peace-filled message, then tripped over his own poetry and faded into the shadows—but whoever the messenger and whatever the message, the war was the subject now.

John came home on the *Gridley* and asked Julia to marry him. But Dick Pershing had done that, too—had left behind a betrothed—and the sadness had been doubled; they agreed to tell almost no one their plans. In November 1968, three months more of training behind him, with twelve hundred Americans dying now every month, he headed back to Vietnam, this time to skipper a boat.

IT'S NOT LIKELY HE WAS EXPECTING any heroics. A Swift Boat, or PCF (for patrol craft fast), was a light, fifty-foot aluminum boat designed originally around its twenty-three-knot speed, as a water taxi to service offshore oil rigs. It had been adapted by the navy for use in coastal patrolling—which is what John expected to be doing: patrolling the coastline of the South China Sea.

John would skipper two of these boats, PCF numbers 44 and 94, beginning in December '68 and lasting most of the next four months. Over the course of these months, under his command or not, many sad, obscene, or heroic things are said to have taken place: an old man tending water buffalo on Christmas Eve shot and killed by a gunner named James Wasser, who says it has spoiled his Christmases ever since; a twelve-year-old boy in a sampan, on the river after curfew, shot to death by the men of PCF 44; a wounded VC soldier carrying a rocket launcher, chased up a beach by John, who then shot him dead as he fled; on a moonless night on the Cua Lon River, after firing on another after-curfew sampan: "the limbs of a small child, limp on the sacks of rice"; another old man, captured by mercenaries, knifed to death then sliced to pieces, his body left with a letter as a warning to the Viet Cong; a Vietnamese woman, taken prisoner from a hut by a river where she had been writing a letter to her boyfriend: "sat very calmly, watching the movements of the men who had just blown four of her countrymen to bits." And James Rassmann, the twenty-one-year-old Special Forces lieutenant knocked from a boat in the Bai Hap River and too weak and exhausted from ducking bullets to do anything but drown, pulled from the water and away from the bullets by the strength of John's one remaining good arm.

John himself is the source for most of these accounts, and for many others like them. Almost from the first day, he kept a journal, which he called his "war notes." Unlike his letters to his parents and to Julia, which are full of the sorts of confusions and anguished recountings you'd expect from a young man new to war, the war notes read more like front-line dispatches, but darker, more self-conscious, more weighted with feeling and mood. He writes of "fish nets dangling from teepee poles . . . swaying to the gentle evening breeze," of water buffalo, "dark, black and strong," rubbing their backs against tree trunks; a dying South Vietnamese soldier—"completely nude, and his bony, minute body stretched out on the brown plastic mat . . . his eyes, only half-open and dazed, searching for something." He describes a woman in a sampan, "hold[ing] her baby tight against bare breast and nipple firm"; helicopters in formation, "ugly and insect-like"; a moment of "hell and blindness [as] the reeds erupt and the bullets walk out across the water."

Much of it is written in the second person, no doubt to heighten the effect. ("You watch for a moment as red streaks move at you in a three-dimensional kaleidoscope.") The writing is sensitive, expressive, even moving—but it's as much a performance as the speech he gave at Yale.

This is the duality that plagues him. This is the enigma, or at least a big part of it. Here you have this stricken, sensitive sailor at war, his oldest friend dead, waste and craziness everywhere he looks—and still he can't take himself out of the spotlight, can't take his eye off posterity to focus on the now. (For all the mood and detail in his Christmas Eve "war notes" entry—the buffalo, the fishnets, the holiday memories of "roast chestnuts and fires with birch logs"—he makes no reference to the old man who was killed.)

But it isn't that he lacked feelings, or that his thoughts or ideals were counterfeit—almost no one who knows him, I think, would claim that. It is only that nothing ever, for John, even in that dark time, has gone deeper than his need to *show himself well*: to achieve, to be accepted, to be revered. The forum almost doesn't matter: school, hockey, war, debating, flying planes. (At St. Paul's, after playing catch with a tennis ball off and on one spring with his roommate, he announced abruptly one day that he had "won." "All spring long," Lew Rutherford would recall later, "John had apparently counted up the times that he had dropped it and I had dropped it. The guy is absolutely *relentless*.")

He's a child this way. He always has been. He tries too hard and cares too much. He puts people off. But that doesn't stop him—he only tries harder. And the distinctions accumulate, along with the disdain. He would win three Purple Hearts in Vietnam, as well as a Silver Star and Bronze Star for gallantry, but all anyone wants to talk about—including two former commanders—is how piddling were his wounds. He killed at least one man, saved the life of another, and lost none of the sailors who served under his command. Most of these men swear he was a good skipper; one or two have called him a hero. But one commanding officer recalls him as "a loose cannon," another describes him as devious and self-absorbed, and a PCF 44 crewmate, Stephen Gardner, has come as close to calling him a coward as he could manage without using the word. He has never been a man who earns admirers easily, or leaves warm feelings in his wake.

THERE WAS AN ARTICLE WRITTEN ABOUT John in *GQ* in early 2006. Based largely on the accounts of unnamed senate aides, former aides, and Democratic "strategists," it painted him, eighteen months after his election loss, as a near-pariah within his party. It was an unkind piece of journalism, I thought, and pretty substanceless. But there is a scene recounted in it that captures perfectly his hard-trying, so often unrequited earnestness—today and forty-five years ago.

It took place, as the writer tells it, on an afternoon in early 2005 on the floor of the Senate before a vote on judicial nominees. A circle of the Senate's top Democrats—Hillary Clinton, Harry Reid, and several others—had formed spontaneously and were talking among themselves. John, at that point only four or five months removed from carrying the party's standard, arrived at the perimeter of the circle and waited for his cue to join in: "But like a cocktail party clique that rejects a dullard, the group didn't part to welcome him. In fact, no one paid him any attention at all."

John stood there for several moments, the writer reports, not knowing quite what to do, then "turned around awkwardly and tugged at his shirtsleeves . . . put his head down and walked away."

That was John at St. Paul's—to a tee. It was also me. I remember those circles that wouldn't open—the Regs, the jocks, and the rest—and the deadening awfulness of standing there, jingling the change in my pockets, trying to look distracted by other, higher things. Those were the moments, in the end, that would drive me inside: toward books and language, dark movies (*The Three Faces of Eve, A Place in the Sun*), the hundred-yard dash—where I needed no one and nothing but my will and my legs—heady friendships with other brooding outsiders, the abstraction of being wildly in love with a succession of girls I barely knew and almost never saw.

It was a kind of self-correcting natural selection: to not go where you weren't welcome or chase what you couldn't possess. And eventually, if you were lucky, as most of us would be, life had a way of landing you more or less where you belonged.

John defied this wisdom. He had no way with people, none at all. His stiffness was a trademark, his insecurities were at least as crippling as mine—a politician's life might have been the *last* career path a wise counselor would have sent him on. But there were all those other pulls: his father's public service, his mother's idealism, the early years in Europe, the shimmering beacon that JFK had become. And a willful self-reliance from all those years alone at boarding schools.

So he pursued. And the pursuit began early, years earlier than for the rest of us. The debate team, the Political Union, the choice of a friend, a roommate, a girlfriend or (ultimately) a wife, the decision to go to war—all these things which, for most of us, were answers to feelings, needs, or preferences or responses to natural gifts, for John were more than that. They were rungs on a ladder, roads taken that would lead to other roads. He was making life choices when the rest of us were still choosing between spring-vacation venues, between the college major we favored and the one that would leave us with more time to go skiing or get laid.

Some would call this opportunism—and still today, if the rumors are true, boo him at class-reunion dinners.

Others would say it's just a matter of going after what you want. Either way, there's something kind of remarkable about it. Something admirable, I think, even if a little sad: forty-five years later, still standing outside the circle, waiting for his time.

Returning

VERY LATE ONE NIGHT IN THE winter of 1978–79, I left a bar on the West Side of Manhattan and drove south on the New Jersey Turnpike toward the suburban town an hour outside the city where I was living alone at the time. It was snowing. I was drunk and lonely, driving as fast as I could, cutting between trailer-trucks, which were the only things left on the road. The speed and the danger excited me, and the night, and the roar of the highway—they seemed to clean out my brain. The snow was coming down in slants. I remember that the road had a sheen.

I was thirty-four, divorced six months, with a two-year-old son I saw nearly every day but still felt a stranger to. Four months before, to fill the hole in my life the wreckage of my marriage had left (though I was still ten years away from seeing the truth of this), I had resurrected the remains of a failed weekly in Atlantic City, which was now eating through my inheritance at the rate of nearly ten thousand dollars a week. My uncle Jack had died of cancer that spring, which felt like the end of a link to something very dear. I had told my sister over dinner that there were times I didn't want to be alive. She had answered that I was feeling sorry for myself, then had gone off with a guy she'd just met shooting pool. But it had felt true to me. It still did. I drove as fast as the road and the snow would let me.

I made it home that night, which I've always thought of as the closest thing to God's doing of anything that's ever happened to me. The Atlantic City weekly would not survive in the end, although there were some nobilities during that long death. It would last long enough, though, to take all the rest of my inheritance, along with four million dollars of other people's money and more than eight years of my life. But there would never be another night quite as dark.

I would meet a woman at the tail-end of that time—an angel to me, though I was still too foolish, and still drinking too much, to see the blessings I had—and would live with her and her two children, in Vermont then Massachusetts, for six mostly very good years. By the time they ended in the early 1990s, I had written two books, a bad one and a better one, and had seen the better one published. A year or so later—I was fifty by that time—I found a home I loved.

It is on the main street of a small town in New Hampshire, a town not so different probably from the farm town in Pennsylvania where Arthur spent his early years. And in this town, every July fourth morning in a field in back of the local bank, two black Hereford bulls are enclosed inside an orange plastic fence. The field is divided into numbered chalk-marked grids; tickets are sold and the small crowd waits outside the plastic. And after a time one of the bulls does its business in one of the grids. There is loud applause; the holder of the winning ticket claims his prize.

The game is called Cow Flop Bingo. It's followed later in the day by a hayride, a sausage roast by the local women's club, a parade of old fire engines, Miss Americas, Uncle Sams, large farm machinery, costumed people on floats, veterans playing calliope music from the backs of antique cars, and the best fireworks for thirty miles around.

The rest of the year the town is very quiet. I came here twelve years ago, left for three years, then came back. There's a good chance I'll die here. It might be the only place I've ever felt at home.

There is a different woman in my life now, closer to its center than any woman has ever been before. I hope that I can hold her there. I don't drink anymore. I hardly gamble. And Sam, the son I had from that long-ago marriage, is no longer the stranger he was. He lives in New York now, as I did at thirty-one, and still has trouble understanding, as I would have then, why exactly I live here, what it is I feel for this town.

But that may be changing. The last time he came to visit, we built a fire in the snow and cooked sausages on a beach at the edge of the lake. He seemed to enjoy that. He seemed to understand more.

THE TOWN, BY PURE COINCIDENCE, is less than thirty minutes northwest of the St. Paul's campus in Concord. And two years ago, on a warm Saturday in early June, I returned for a visit there. It was graduation weekend, the school's 150th. Except for a three-month stint as a visiting teacher five or six winters before, I hadn't been on the campus since the afternoon I left it, more or less in disgrace, in June of 1961.

It was still early, an hour before the start of things. The campus was quiet, but ready: new-mowed grass as far as you could see, the elms ringed with fresh plantings, window boxes heavy with color. Students, boys and girls, walked in pairs or in threes, laughing and talking, feckless for the first time since winter. A group of boys in shorts and T-shirts, all about sixteen, were tossing a tennis ball across the grass median that divides the footpath from the road—rarely used—that runs the length of the campus. A throw missed its target, and landed, bouncing, near my feet. I kicked it, a sideways kick, soccer-style, toward the nearest boy, who was waiting a few feet away. I missed completely—the ball kept rolling—then, with my right foot half in the air, I twisted, staggered, and almost fell.

The boy was there in an instant, seeming ready to catch me. "You okay, sir?" he asked, but with less urgency than politeness. I said that I was. He smiled pleasantly, rescued the ball from under the bush where it had landed, and threw it back to his friends in the road.

I was alone, and glad of it. I wandered: down past what used to be the Lower School Fields, where John had asked for my vote all those years ago on our way back to the lockers; then left the path and crossed two other fields, where I'd played soccer for three autumns, passing by Memorial Hall, where the third-form photo had been taken—I thought of stopping on its steps, the same steps, but I didn't—then through the quad where I'd lived, sullen and roommate-less, for my third- and fourth-form years; and finally back to the main campus and into the old dining hall, which was now a gallery exhibiting student art. I had looked for the track but couldn't find it. The old Lower, where I'd spent my first year at the school—the loneliest, scariest year of my life—had been gone twenty years by now, razed to make way for a glass-sided library with open-space reading rooms flooded in natural light.

OUTSIDE THE CHAPEL, ON THE GRASS across from the rectory, a crowd is gathering for the alumni parade. It isn't a large crowd—the parade itself will be larger—mostly just faculty, family, and a scattering of students, two or three hundred at most. On the chapel lawn, three boys are throwing a Frisbee. Two more are wrestling as a girl watches; the boy on the bottom, in a headlock, shrieks in mock pain. The girl laughs. No one else seems to notice or to care.

It is the seventy-fifth anniversary of the class of 1931. There are three of them. They are at the head of the parade, in a golf cart with a younger man at the wheel. All three men are thin and pale, in ties and jackets with straw boaters on their heads and small plastic tags in their lapels. One of them is holding a placard—'31—which he waves weakly from time to time. All three are smiling, moving their heads from side to side, rhythmically, like beauty queens, acknowledging the quiet claps from either side of the road. They look wonderfully happy, but also impossibly frail.

Next is the class of 1936. All four members—it is their seventieth, so they are around eighty-eight—walk under their own power, two with the help of canes, another guided by a daughter, moving slowly but surely behind the seventy-fifth anniversary cart.

And so they pass, at five-year intervals: the ancient followed by the old followed by the elderly, in carts, on walkers, in wheelchairs, and on canes, some leaning on relatives, the hardier ones powering themselves. Their faces are road maps, of lives well and poorly lived: marriages, divorces, work, illness, the joys of family, the wages of liquor, fortunes made or misspent.

With each new class that passes—'41, '46, '51, my older brothers' era, and then, with the sixties, my own—the numbers grow larger, the movements spryer, the postures more erect. With '76 come the first females (the school went coed in '72): trim, comely, middle-aged women in Capri pants and sandals and pulled-back hair. There are black faces now, too, and Asian ones—unthinkable in my time—and then there are more, and the Capri pants turn to culottes, then to shorts; the hair grows shaggier, the faces blanker; the boaters turn to baseball caps—maroon, with SPS in white letters over the bill—the ties and jackets disappear. Then there are toddlers, skipping alongside parents in Yankees T-shirts; then infants in strollers, backpacks, ponytails, ripped blue jeans, miniskirts, weird sunglasses, halter tops with cleavage, bottles of Heineken and Poland Spring. An hour later, in the buffet line on the chapel lawn, an alumnus, back for his fortieth—his first reunion, he will tell me, since his fifth—will stand looking at the passing scene, then turn to a friend and shake his head—"Can you *believe* this shit?"

MY LAST STOP IS THE CHAPEL. It hasn't changed. There is no changing such a thing. Dark and massive and purposefully august, built in the school's earliest days, in the English Gothic tradition—its 120-foot tower dwarfing everything in sight—it is far less church than cathedral. I think this now; I never would have then: an

English cathedral in a small New Hampshire field. Set back from the road by its two hundred feet of lawn, its rear side close enough to the pond behind so that its tower casts a reflection halfway to the far shore, it seems designed to dominate: both the landscape and the memories of grown men.

I enter it as I always did, as we *all* did: through the gray-stone, windowed hallway that used to connect to the study hall—the Big Study—next door. The Big Study is gone now, gone in the fire of our fifth-form year. But the hallway—the smell, the vague dankness, the feeling—is the same. The only difference is the backpacks: eight or nine of them in a line along the floor, their books and water bottles and a pair of lacrosse gloves jammed into side pockets, left there, I can only think, to keep the water cool.

On both sides of the chapel doorway are lined the memorial tablets, some nearly as old as the school. Lloyd's uncle's is there, a three-foot, deep-carved rectangular inscription ("With Enduring Love . . . Killed in Action over Guam . . ."), exactly at eye-level, just to the left of the doors. It is as unfamiliar to me as all of the others—and I wonder, reading it now for the first time, how often Lloyd, in his four years of passing it daily, allowed himself ten seconds alone with its message. Or if he ever did.

The Angel of Death is still here, in the antechapel with her naked soldier—they are the first thing I see after coming through the doors. Then the altar, all the way in the distance at the end. It is a long walk from one to the other, if you walk it slowly. And I do. And the old feelings are there, or some of them. Along with a powerful urge to kneel.

But also, in the sudden dark coming in from the sunlight, and the damp cool from the summer air outside, there is something else, too: relief, a sense of respite, that I'd never noticed—or needed—as a boy.

THE LAWN OUTSIDE IS FULL NOW with the lunch crowd—I can hear them if I let myself. There is no one but me in the chapel. I am in a choir pew just down from the altar: the same pew I sat in as a second-form soprano, and chose for organ recitals after Sunday evensongs. The organ is just across from me, close enough to see every pipe. The choir room is behind me, six paces and two stair steps away. It is all very near. And at this moment, for the first time, very precious.

Without this past year, without Arthur and the emails and the meetings, it would probably still seem near to me—memory, with the right promptings, can always be made to collapse life. But it would not have the preciousness. It would only seem strange then to be here, strange and a little frightening, with only the old fears and loneliness to sit with me in this pew.

It began with the photograph, which I think of now sitting here, and the boy with the screwed-up look, who seemed only a silly stranger. And the others, my classmates, only ciphers. There are no strangers or ciphers anymore.

I think of Philip, a stranger then but now a friend, and of the sunny March morning three months before in his apartment in New York. We had been talking since I got there about what it means to be connected—to a church, a lover, to each other—and what happens when the connections are severed or lost. At St. Paul's, Philip had said, the connections had mostly to do with the miseries we shared. But they were no less strong for that.

"There was an *isolation*. A constant, daily isolation. They enforced it. They choreographed it. The method was to enclose you, to keep you from the world, to keep you locked up in that dark, beautiful place, isolated, subjected to its parts—chapel, classes, sports, tradition, all those things that would turn you into a *Christian gentleman* . . .

"But there was *community* in all that isolation. We ate together, slept together, worshipped together, there was nothing we didn't share. The more coldness, the greater the isolation—the more of a community we were."

This sounded right to me, and I told him so. A second later, out of absolutely nowhere, he asked me: "Do you remember the evensong prayer?" And I answered that yes, of course I did—although it had been years since I'd said it or heard it, and even as I answered I wasn't certain of myself.

And Philip smiled and recited the first line, and before he had finished, the words were back with me as though they had never been gone. And I understood perfectly why he had asked. I joined with him on the second line and we recited it through together to the end.